D0052289

WORK

WORK

MAKING A LIVING AND
MAKING A LIFE

JOSHUA HALBERSTAM, PH.D.

A PERIGEE BOOK

A Perigee Book
Published by The Berkley Publishing Group
A division of Penguin Putnam Inc.
375 Hudson Street
New York, New York 10014

First edition: April 2000

Published simultaneously in Canada.

The Penguin Putnam Inc. World Wide Web site address is
http://www.penguinputnam.com

Library of Congress Cataloging-in-Publication Data

Halberstam, Joshua, 1946–
Work: making a living and making a life / Joshua Halberstam.— 1st ed.
p. cm.
Includes index.
ISBN 0-399-52578-5
1. Work—Psychological aspects. 2. Job enrichment. 3. Conduct of life. 4.
Motivation (Psychology) I. Title: Making a living and making a life. II. Title.

BF481 .H33 2000
158.7—dc21   99-057671
CIP

Printed in the United States of America

10 9 8 7 6 5 4 3 2 1

For my sister, Rivy

WORK

CONTENTS

Contents

ACKNOWLEDGMENTS

THEN and again, philosophers have had something to say about *work*. Not surprisingly, the nitty-gritty demands of everyday business and work life are not what engages their professional interest. Their concerns are more abstract, directed to the broader social commentary. Business analysts, on the other hand, generally stay away from theoretical concerns with the "meaning of work" and focus, rather, on "practicalities." Their everyday issues can range from advice for managers and entrepreneurs to detailed recipes for career planning.

It's been clear to me for some time that we need to bridge the divide between these two domains. This realization was borne of my atypical professional experience. I've spent the bulk of my adult years as a professor of philosophy, but for more than a decade now, I've also been actively involved in business ventures—primarily as a marketing consultant with a few entrepreneurial adventures along the way. Philosophy and business? You bet. Marketing Spinoza to college students is not, marketing-wise, that different than marketing business ideas to clients. They both involve stripping away assumptions so that old problems can be viewed afresh. Unexpected solutions invariably follow.

Philosophy also has something to say about values, and

values are crucial in our work and careers. This isn't empty rhetoric or moral posturing. When business people talk about the "bottom line" they usually mean the profit-loss at the end of a venture. But, in fact, the financial summation is not the bottom line—there's more below. We bring to our endeavors a host of presumptions about the importance of money, status, power, and work. We have personal standards for what we're willing to trade away for these benefits in the way of our integrity and joy, our creativity and dignity. The bottom line is our lives and all the components that feed into our assessment of its success or failure.

The problem is that these philosophical assumptions are often buried deep in our consciousness, unnoticed and unevaluated. The aim of this book is to make those implicit assumptions explicit, to bring them out into the open where they can be examined and reconsidered. As we shall see, with the emergence of our global, high-tech, knowledge-based economy, the need for this kind of analysis is more important than ever. As our careers increasingly become our own responsibility and the private work distinction dissolves, it's critical that we have a better understanding of our genuine ambitions, what we really care about, and how work fits into this bigger picture. And we have to undertake this reexamination with rigor, honesty and without losing our sense of humor.

A word about presentation. A book about how to make a life and how to make a living covers pretty much the whole human enterprise. The full spectrum of scholarship weighs in on this subject. Writing this book, therefore, kept me busy in the library, moving from journals on psychology and neurology to philosophy and anthropology, to labor history and business studies. But you won't find here a parade of footnotes and citations. I did not want this to be an academic text. The subject is too immediately important for too many of us to be weighed down with academic references, complex syntax, and scholarly jargon.

When you write a book with a subject this broad, you also incur a debt of thanks to lots of people. Friends and colleagues allowed me to badger them with questions and provided me with eye-opening insights into their work lives. I thank them all for their patience and honesty. A special thanks to Shimon Neustein for our conversations about work and his provocative ideas about creative work and theology. The book owes its creation, as well, to the efforts of my agent, Agnes Birnbaum, the editorial staff at Perigee Books, a division of Penguin Putnam Inc., and, especially, the editorial wizardry of Irene Prokop. My wife, Yoco, and the kids indulged my work on the "work book" with their usual understanding and encouragement. The book is dedicated to my sister, Rivy, who has been a cheerful cheerleader of my writing career and who, I want to remind her, will always be older than me.

An Ancient Indian Legend

Soon after humans were created, the gods held an extraordinary meeting among themselves. They had an urgent problem to consider. Human beings must never discover the secret of life, they agreed, but where could they hide the secret so that it remained safely hidden forever?

"At the top of the very highest mountains," one god suggested early in the discussion. "Humans can't climb that high." But the gods quickly dismissed this proposal. "They can't now," they said, "but perhaps they will learn to do so in the future."

For this reason, too, the gods rejected the idea of hiding the secret of life in the depths of the ocean. "Humans are imaginative creatures," they noted, "and someday they may invent the means to survey even the ocean floor." And so the gods considered one plan after another without success until, finally, one god came up with the perfect solution.

"Bury the secret of life in their hearts. They will never think to look there."

And so they did.

CHAPTER ONE

The New Career—Entrepreneur

> No other technique for the conduct of life
> attaches the individual so firmly to reality as
> laying emphasis on work; for his work at least
> gives him a secure place in a portion of reality,
> in the human community.
>
> —Sigmund Freud

> It's true hard work never killed anybody, but
> I figure, why take the chance?
>
> —Ronald Reagan

ONE evening, on an otherwise quiet, uneventful walk, the problem long lurking in a crevice of your mind finally grabs and holds your attention. It is time to take stock.

Fact: You spend the major portion of your life's waking hours dealing with work. Sure, you think about the details of your job all the time, but the concern here is the much bigger picture. Does your career connect with how you envision your life? Yes, you need the money, and no, this isn't an adolescent call to chuck your job and hop on the next train to the hills of New Mexico, nor is it some great defect of character to look forward to a step up in the car you drive. But this evening, you want to get beyond these diversions and on to the more intimate relationship between you and your work. "So tell me," you ask yourself, slowing your pace, "how much sheer joy do I have on most days in the office? What if my salary were determined by how much pleasure I received from doing my job? At the end of the day, does my work make me feel ennobled or degraded?"

Beware before you rush to answer: It's more socially acceptable to complain about your job than to admit to enjoying it. Either way, do you have a clear sense of what aspect of your work provides the greatest highs? And speaking of highs, what about the hours you aren't working—are you satisfied with the way you spend your leisure time? "Heavy" questions indeed, and scary ones—though not to ask them and, instead, to proceed with your work life, carried forward only by inertia, is even scarier.

As we begin the twenty-first century, we find ourselves in the throes of a curious combination of exhaustion and restlessness. Most of us work hard, most of us are tired too much of the time, but most of us are also a bit frantic. If pressed, we can't say exactly what makes it all worth it. For, as prosaic as it sounds, work does nourish us, but only when it is part of a larger, richer context. We resonate to this reminder because somewhere deep in our gut we do understand that more purchasing power isn't what fulfills us in the end. What, then, does?

It takes work to find out. We won't find the answer in lofty slogans such as "Find your inner self," or "Turn the profane into the sacred." Will the savants who issue these rhetorical bumper stickers pay our mortgage this month? We need to make a living in the hard-boiled streets of the marketplace, not on secluded, mystical mountaintops. We want an approach to our work life that reflects the big human picture, but also reflects the reality that pays the rent.

Walking away from these questions will no longer be an option. In the old days when you had this heart-to-heart conversation with yourself, you could shrug it off the next morning. You had a job to do, a career to pursue, and little time for philosophical explorations of the meaning of work; it wasn't as if you had much choice about the matter anyway. Now, the twenty-first century greets us with a cryptic smile as it introduces us to our new work environment. From now on, we will have no choice but to make choices. Like it or not, we will all become entrepreneurs of our careers; our careers will become, literally, our own business. Our work lives will be our responsibility: to create, manage, market, and sustain. Work will be permanently temporary; we will no longer "have jobs" as we did in the past, but "do jobs." Private life and work life will merge, so that what counts as "making it" will be a personal choice as well.

This transformation will be a liberating opportunity for some, and a complex challenge for all. To flourish in this new environment, we must have the one element we sorely lack. We need a new work ethic. The one we have no longer works.

The introduction to this book retells a legend about "the secret of life." I have no idea what the secret might be, or even whether such a thing could exist, but the fable does point to a curious feature of human behavior. We persist in looking for solutions to problems outside our own experience, and presume that truths flourish only across the border. One "secret of life"— and this is also the secret of creativity and productive thinking—is to express, as honestly as you can, what is in your own heart. The visionary, the person with insight, is the one who sees what is before his own eyes.

I, for one, don't see much value in work as some obligatory service, be it to God, king, or global economy. The richest rewards of work, I believe, are right there in the doing. When work has integrity; when it is creative, fertile, elegant, and engaging; when it is connected to our leisure; and when it is part of a worthy larger social enterprise, then the endeavor is its own reward.

The target here, accordingly, is a philosophical understanding of work that, by implication, can change the way we understand and pursue our lives. We begin that journey with a splash of cold reality, an overview of the new American way of work, how it got to be what it is, and where it is headed tomorrow.

HAVING JOBS, DOING JOBS: SOME HISTORY

> [I]n a fast-moving economy, jobs are rigid solutions to an elastic problem. Jobs are no longer socially adaptive. . . . That is why they are going the way of the dinosaur.
> —William Bridges, *JobShift*

My formula for success. Rise early, work late, strike oil.
—J. P. Getty

In soloing—as in other activities—it is easier to start some-thing than to finish it.

—Amelia Earhart

We imagine that people always had jobs. Not so. Human beings have always worked hard, all right—except, of course, the idle rich drinking tea in their parlors, gazing out their windows to observe "their workers" at toil. But the hard work was primarily task-oriented: hunt the caribou, construct a house, sow that field, mend the boots. Whether one worked alone or with others, going to work meant doing specific chores as the day or season determined.

The word *job* itself reaches back to before the Renaissance and derives from the word *gob*, which meant "a small piece" (a lump, a mouthful). *Job* later referred to larger pieces of stuff, and later still to the act of transporting that larger pile. Eventually the word came to denote any task that was a single piece of work. Jobbers were and are "pieceworkers." When we report that Harry gave the printing job to Larry, who felt good about the job he did, while Larry stayed at home to complete the awful job of cleaning out the front closet, we're using the word *job* in this older sense of an assigned piece of work.

The piecemeal job as the standard for how people made their living came to an end in the nineteenth century with the appearance of the steam engine and the parade of inventions marching behind it. Industrialization arrived and work was transformed. In the preindustrial world, jobs were activities; now they were positions. People no longer *did* jobs but *had* jobs. And with industrialization, jobs became slaves to the hour. In previous centuries, the weather and the length of daylight governed the work schedule, but thanks to electrical lighting and efficient time-pieces, companies were suddenly able to make sure employees showed up "on time" and that production continued around the clock. The demands of manufacturing also brought workers into organizations for lifetime employment and thereby created a new situation: If you had a job, you could lose it. You could become one of the "unemployed." A new insecurity was born.

By the middle of the twentieth century having a job wasn't enough: People also wanted a career. The promise of security that came with a structured career path had a special appeal, especially to children of the Depression entering the workforce in the 1950s. Contrary to current popular myth, even fifty years ago Americans did considerable job-hopping, but most did intend to spend their entire work life at one company. They expected to have a career of continuous upward mobility, to reap the benefits of seniority, and for the most ambitious, to get a crack at the top of the ladder.

You can now kick away the ladder. It no longer leads anywhere. The postindustrial world taking shape in the twenty-first century flips the definition of the *job* yet again. We're going back to doing jobs, not having jobs. The reformulation has been under way for some time. In the

United States today, the average worker will have had ten employers over the course of his work life. For all workers, the average tenure of employment at one company is just four and a half years—and for managers and professionals just six years. While job tenure in the United States is the shortest of any industrialized nation, the pattern is increasingly global. *Shuushin koyoo seido*, as they call it in Japan, is the venerated notion that company and employee share mutual, immutable, everlasting loyalty to one another. The reality is otherwise: Japanese companies now routinely lay off staff and actively encourage early retirement, especially of their women employees. Over the span of a work life, the average contemporary Japanese employee now has six different employers.

What happened? The metamorphosis of jobs is the result of the convergence of many developments. We can group these factors into three broad categories.

The global economy

Look at the label on your shirt. Does it say Made in Malaysia? Made in Hong Kong? Made in the Philippines? It probably doesn't say Made in the USA. Manufacturing is now worldwide, markets are everywhere, and as American companies have learned, some too late, if you sit on your fat haunches with your back to the rest of the world, before too long you'll be cavorting with the dodo and the Edsel in the fields of the extinct. To compete in the new planetary playground, you had to become leaner and meaner in a hurry. And so began a frenzy of revamping, reinvention, and reengineering. Companies became voracious predators, acquiring other companies only to spit them out after sucking their juices dry. In a procession of shotgun corporate marriages, companies hurriedly merged; in the period 1990–92 there were more than a thousand mergers in the defense industry alone. Jobs were cast off as a result: Mergers and acquisitions resulted in redundancies, and redundancies resulted in layoffs. (The consultant asks a woman in her office what she does there. "Nothing," she answers. He asks a fellow in the next office what he does, and he, answers, "Nothing at all." "I see," says the consultant. "More redundancy.") Companies also learned to outsource, to hire outsiders with targeted expertise to do the accounting, to run the mailroom and copying operations, and to perform many other jobs that used to be done internally. Outsourcing, too, translates into fewer permanent jobs.

The financial conclusion was readily apparent: The future security of the corporation meant less job security for its employees.

Technology

In a world where everything could be done by machinery, everything would be done by machinery.
—George Orwell

Picture a worker. Are you imagining a man in a factory, muscles taut, beads of sweat dripping down his face, as he manipulates a heavy sheet of steel? This icon belongs in the classics section of the gallery, for the representative worker of today looks nothing like this. As Shoshana Zuboff observes in *In the Age of the Smart Machine,* something new exists between the worker and his product: data. The modern workplace has become, in her phrase, "informated." The contemporary steel mill laborer is more likely to manipulate sheets of paper than sheets of steel, more likely to move a computer mouse than a hammer, and "he" might well be a "she." Indeed, if you want a representative picture of the contemporary worker, leave the steel mill altogether and walk down the block to an office building, because most people now work not with things but with information: creating it, transforming it, selling it, servicing it.

According to the Bureau of Labor Statistics, by the mid-1990s more Americans were working in computer-related businesses than in automobile-related businesses, more in biotechnology than in machine-tool industries, more in surgical and medical concerns than in plumbing or heating. In 1950, 60 percent of all jobs in the United States were unskilled, but by 1995, unskilled labor was down to 25 percent of the labor force, and will drop to as low as 15 percent as we begin the twenty-first century. The industrial worker is rapidly being replaced by the postindustrial worker whose product is not things but knowledge.

In a technologically driven, knowledge-rich business, location—the workplace—matters less and less. Thanks to faxes, modems, Web sites, and cellular phones, your office can now be your hotel room, your bedroom, your car, or a lounge chair on the beach. By the mid-1990s, tens of millions of workers were telecommuting from their homes during regular business hours. Companies encouraged this new, ubiquitous workplace, handing out laptop computers to their employees so that they could work wherever they found themselves.

These technological changes undermine the need for the traditional full-time, permanent job site. The chief concern of the contemporary manager is to get the project in on time and in good shape, and she doesn't much care that one member of her team claims to be inspired by leprechauns from Mars, and another says he's most productive when working at home at three in the morning, wearing pajamas and a top hat. The project is supreme, not the time sheet, not the location.

When jobs are cast as projects, job descriptions don't matter much. Any such description has a fleeting shelf life in our postindustrial world of just-in-time production, rapidly mutating goals, and shifting global markets.

The new worker

The demands of global business and technological innovations in production are just part of the reason jobs are no longer what they were. Another crucial factor is a new attitude toward work among workers. Social theorists keep busy trotting out reasons for this development. Current favorite hypotheses include "the feminization of the workplace," the maturing baby boomers' residual distaste for authority, a general societal emphasis on personal autonomy and aversion to paternalism, and the growing interest in entrepreneurship. No doubt each tells part of the story, but a particularly illuminating way to make sense of the evolution in worker expectations is to examine the perspective not of the employee but of the employer.

Meet Federick Winslow Taylor. Taylor was the brilliant late-nineteenth-century innovator whose enduring influence on management has been compared with that of Marx and Freud. Dedicated to the notion that the scientific standards of exactness and quantification should apply to all spheres of our lives, Taylor was especially impatient with the "messy" operation of workers in the manufacturing industries, and in response developed a model for the management of efficient labor. He called this approach "scientific management." The chief novelty was to rigorously connect time with production. By mechanizing motion down to its smallest movements, he could get workers, interchangeable cogs in the vast manufacturing machine, to do more in less time; as a result, employers produced more, made more money, and could pay their workers more.

Taylor was unabashed in his paternalism toward workers. Brink Lindsey, in an article in *Reason* magazine, reports that Taylor commonly told laborers, "You are not supposed to think. There are people paid for thinking around here." The role of workers, he insisted, was "to do what they are told to do promptly and without asking questions and making suggestions." After all, as he explained, anyone "sufficiently phlegmatic and stupid" to choose handling pig iron for a living is "rarely able to comprehend the science of handling pig iron." This management philosophy splendidly achieved its goals, and soon factories everywhere began to monitor worker output and institute regimes to eliminate wasted motions. Taylorism was the model that inspired Ford Motor Company's innovative use of assembly lines to mass-produce cars.

This managerial attitude couldn't, however, last for long. Resentment toward the harsh coldness of efficiency grew quickly, sometimes finding artistic outlets, as in the bitter humor of Charlie Chaplin's film *Modern Times*. But the seed for change by corporate owners wasn't so much a sudden surge of moral qualms as the realization that treating people as unmotivated machines no longer made business sense. Strict Taylorism is productive when you're dealing with slaves in the field or rows of laborers in a factory and you don't care what these people think. It fails, however, when the worker's brawn is less valuable than his brains. As workers' collars changed from the blue of the first half of the twentieth century to the gray and white of the second half of the century, Taylorism faded in the bleach.

The Japanese were the first to discard the Taylor top-down management approach in favor of the "enlightened" bottom-up approach. Rebuilding their shattered economy after World War II, they discovered the ideas of W. Edwards Deming, an American who was thoroughly ignored in his own country. Total Quality, as this approach is sometimes called, assumes that workers do care about quality, not just their wages, and that their input into the process of production is a significant factor in the outcome. Managers were now told to respect employee autonomy and responsibility. The management mantra of "empower-ment" was introduced in the 1980s in the United States, and continues on into the next century.

What followed from this noble sentiment? Like an overly fertile fungus, the quality approach to management mushroomed into an endless variety of management pro-grams and corresponding slogans of the week. We were introduced to theory Y, the replacement for theory X, and then went on to the management by objectives models of theory Z. Quality circles were formed to attain the goal of zero defect manufacturing. Total Quality Management had its long fifteen minutes of fame, stooping to remind secretaries to answer the phone before the third ring. Reengineering then became the battle cry of companies as they marched to cut out globs of middle management along with unused inventory. Mission-and-vision pro-grams talked about corporate culture and values, and cor-porations redefined themselves as learning organizations. Team approaches were designed to flatten chains of com-mand. Perhaps in reaction to all this activity, Peter Drucker, the foremost U.S. management theorist, says that he'd prefer to give up the word *management* altogether because it implies subordinates. He finds himself using executive more, because it implies responsibility for an area, not necessarily dominion over people.

But call it what you will—no one is fooling anyone. Taylorism is hardly extinct. Encouraging employee think-ing is certainly more considerate than treating people like equipment, but both employers and employees know who works for whom, who has dominion and who does not.

Executives or managers are advised to "empower workers" because it makes financial sense to raise morale in order to raise profits. In fact, the careful monitoring of workers is now far more "scientific" than Taylor could ever have imagined.

Meanwhile, the new workers have become more vocal about their own bottom line. Family matters now matter. Nearly nine out of ten American workers are part of a family, and when the New York Family and Work Institute conducted a national study of what workers cared about, more than half rated family-support policies of employers as key in their decision to accept a particular job; 60 percent of the respondents rated the effect of a job on their personal life as much more important than wages, benefits, and even job security.

Perhaps the most powerful factor in the shift in attitude is the massive entry of women into the workforce in the last quarter of the twentieth century. This infusion has had dramatic consequences. As women settle into the nation's offices, factories, and medical centers, they bring a new set of expectations about the role of the job in one's life. The traditional career path is not usually part of the package.

All histories, of course, are more than just the flow of events. They also include the flow of ideas that propel and respond to those events. The concept of work has had its own stormy history, one we need to examine as we chart our own views about the role of work in our lives.

HAVING JOBS, DOING JOBS: SOME PHILOSOPHY

Philosophers and their fellow travelers—theologians, social critics, thinkers-at-large—don't do much work in the traditional sense, but this hardly stops them from having a lot to say about the subject. In truth, work does raise fundamental questions about human life and how we choose to spend it: Is work fundamentally enriching or demoralizing? Is it a value we should encourage, or an oppression we should strive to eliminate? The opposing answers have sustained an argument for thousands of years.

As you might expect, the debate usually begins with a prior exchange over the meaning of the word *work*. Work has been characterized, for example, as active, in contrast, say, to lying on a beach—unless, of course, the person on the beach is a doctor on call. But what about a game of Ping-Pong? That's not just lying around, but it isn't work either . . . unless, of course, you're a professional Ping-Pong player. Is payment, then, the criterion for work? Surely not—doing the laundry isn't work. Is it?

This semantic dispute isn't unimportant, because the connotations associated with work have an enormous influence on how we think about our jobs. For example, the English word *travail* comes from the French word for work and refers to agonizing labor, and we still associate work with doing something unpleasant, painful . . . a travail. But even more important than linguistic history in shaping our attitude toward work is our cultural heritage. Our approach to work is always framed in one ideological framework or another. To better figure out what attitude we want to adopt for the future, let's briefly recount some of the more major changes in the Western approach to work.

There's no better place to start a review of Western civilization than with the ancient Greeks. They despised work . . . not just doing work but the idea of it. A free individual of an enlightened mind had better things to do with his time, they insisted. If work you must, and a sorry necessity that, the best you could do to preserve your dignity was subsistence farming. Working for others was pathetic, a form of slavery. The Romans shared this contempt. Sloshing about in their bathhouses, deep in conversation about the politics of empires and the meaning of life, they proclaimed manual labor to be the province of those who couldn't manage the higher pursuits of thought.

The Bible, on the other hand, offered a more complex attitude toward work. In Genesis 2:15, work is portrayed as man's noble calling: "The Lord took the man and placed him in the Garden of Eden to work it and to guard it." Through work, man participates in God's creation; the name Adam traces to the Assyrian Adamu, meaning "maker" or "craftsman." Later, in Isaiah 2:4, a prophecy presents a vision of the end of days, in which mankind is rid of war and returns to its original vocation of work without strife: "They will beat their swords into plowshares and their spears in pruning hooks." But between these blissful bookends of history, work is a curse. Expelled from paradise, Adam will eat only by the sweat of his brow. People will bend their backs under scorching suns and raised whips, not to assist in God's creation but simply to survive. Work is both a blessing and a curse.

The emergent Christian perspective eventually emphasized the view of labor as a religious virtue. This perspective took time to develop. While the Greek and Roman thinkers disparaged work as a distraction from the more noble discourse of ideas, the early church fathers scorned work as a distraction from piety. Augustine, for example, starkly contrasts the base inferiority of labor with the glorious contemplation of the divine. So, too, the early monasteries stipulated that monks undertake only those chores that allowed them to recite the psalms as they went about their assignments. The point of work was not production but obedience. A typical cloister rule of the period asserts that no monk may practice a skill except those whose faith has been proven and who do their work for the benefit of the monastery.

Later Christianity, however, elevated work into exemplary acts of spiritual devotion. The monastic orders now taught that labor was a service to God, particularly the toil of farmers and artisans whose creative production mimes the image of God the creator. In his thoughtful book on the importance of work in contemporary Christianity, *The Reinvention of Work*, Matthew Fox quotes the fourteenth-century mystic Julian of Norwich and notes the connection Julian draws between tilling the land and religious sacrifice:

> *Be a gardener. Dig a ditch, toil and sweat, and turn the earth upside down and seek the deepness and water the*

*plants in time. Continue this labor and make sweet floods
to run and noble and abundant fruits to spring. Take this
food and drink and carry it to God as your true worship.*

But it was the Protestant Reformation that ratcheted up
work to a central position in the religious life of all
Christians. John Calvin went further in this direction than
anyone, preaching the virtues of material success combined
with austere living and hard work. For Calvin, neither
leisure nor enjoyment, but only activity serves to increase
the glory of God. The Calvinist work ethic taught that one
does not work in order to live, but one lives in order to
work; when there is no more to do, it is time for sleep.

In his classic book *The Protestant Ethic and the Spirit
of Capitalism*, published in 1905, Max Weber chronicled
the fertile marriage of the Protestant devotion to hard
work and spare consumption with the ethos of modern
capitalism. The Puritans planted this work ethic in the
New World, where it grew into the ideological staple of
American business.

This stark view of hard work for its own sake is utterly
unappealing to most of us. We aren't wild about the "austere living" part of the project either. But many do agree
with that perspective's underlying tenet: Work gives our
lives meaning. Interestingly, the most vocal advocates for
this view come from opposite ends of the ideological
spectrum. In his encyclical, *Laborem Exercens*, Pope
John Paul II articulated the Catholic view that work is a
distinctive human activity, for it is "one of the character-
istics that distinguishes man from the rest of crea-

tures. . . . Only man is capable of work. . . . Thus work bears the particular mark of man and humanity." At the other end of the theological spectrum, Karl Marx also describes work as man's essential activity and meaningful work as the cornerstone of a flourishing life. Echoing this sentiment, contemporary social critic Daniel Bell argues in his influential book, *The End of Ideology*, that work "always stood at the center of moral consciousness," and we abandon it at our peril.

The opposing approach views work as a curse. True, the affliction of labor is easing as technology removes the necessity for the brutal and dulling toil that consumed most human beings for most of their history. And while work is still no delight for most people on the planet, fewer undergo the pervasive indignities of the past. Nevertheless, insists the anti-work camp, we still have a long, long way to go before we reach our destination: the elimination of work entirely. Work, the late social philosopher Herbert Marcuse claimed, is inherently oppressive, a restraint on our freedom. The goal, therefore, is to have all physical needs accounted for, so that we can return to the idyllic life of leisure suggested by our forebears in classical Greece.

Here, then, are two antithetical views of the role of work and leisure in our lives. Wisdom points to an embrace of both. Leisure is not only a luxury but also, as we shall see in a later chapter, essential to a complete life. But leisure receives its value only when it is the culmination of work that precedes it—work and leisure are a complementary pair. But not just any work will do. Work, just for the sake of work, is useless sweat. Our occupation must be more than simply a way to occupy ourselves.

ON MEANINGFUL WORK

What is not worth doing is not worth doing well.
—Abraham Maslow

We can distinguish what we do as either self-directed or other-directed work. Self-directed work flows from our own choices and reflects our own values. You do your job the way you do because this is who you are—its fits your style, your sense of how it is best accomplished, with the appropriate degree of input from others. Other-directed work is labor that you are constrained to undertake, for it does not correspond to your own goals and interests. Slavery is the most extreme example of other-directed work, but working purely for the money is in the same category.

No work is pure—all work is a mixture of these two types. Even the most exciting, autonomous vocation has its stretches of mundane chores dictated by Mother Nature and human bosses and clients. The institution-free novelist must spend the morning ordering a new cartridge for his printer and wait in line at the post office for stamps. No matter what you do, expect long patches of mindless routine. The critical difference is what leads and what supports: Is your work primarily self-directed or other-directed?

Self-directed work is work we choose to do, but some people have thought, and many still do, that the work chooses us. They insist that each person has his or her work of destiny.

If a man is called to be a street sweeper, he should sweep streets even as Michelangelo painted, or Beethoven played music, or Shakespeare wrote poetry. He should sweep so well that all the hosts of heaven and earth will pause to say, here, lived a great street sweeper who did his job well.
—Martin Luther King, Jr.

If only God would give me a sign—like making a large deposit in my name to a Swiss bank.
—Woody Allen

If only choosing a career were that simple. That's why I envy Estelle. I wish I had her focus. You periodically run into people like her, individuals who seem always to have known exactly what they want to do with their lives. Estelle says she remembers visiting a museum as a child, finding herself fascinated by a work by Van Gogh, and understanding then and there that she was meant to be a painter, too. And she is. You find folks with this sort of relentless determination in the arts, business, teaching, medicine, sports—indeed, the entire gamut of professions.

Estelle's devotion to art is what the earlier Protestant tradition deemed a *beruf* or "calling." Your life had some special task to fulfill, ordained by God just for you. The nature of that task, however, is not always immediately apparent, so you have to listen for the call (our word *vocation* comes from *vocare*, "to call"). A few heed the call, many do not.

We've retained this notion of a predestined calling in our secular occupations. At the age of fifteen, John Stuart Mill was so inspired by the works of his father's philosopher friend, Jeremy Bentham, that he decided on the true objective of his life: to reform the world. Though an agnostic, he borrowed religious language to describe his dedication as a sacred mission. Today, too, some people feel "summoned" to devote their lives to a cause, be it as a relief organizer helping to improve the lives of the downtrodden, or as a bomb builder in the service of a terrorist cadre. But people regularly describe their work as a calling even when it's not as grandiose as reforming the world, producing great art, or for that matter, wreaking havoc on innocent human beings. They speak this way about doing carpentry, owning a shoe store, playing baseball, or performing magic tricks at preschool birthday parties. It isn't the type of work that matters, but the pull it has on one's life.

These callings often first appear after many false starts. The woman who sells me the tulips at the florist shop tells me her story. "I worked as a medical technician, a bookkeeper in a travel agency, in a nursery school, and before that, I even did oil changes and tuned up cars in a garage. Honey, I did all sorts of things. Then I took this course in flower arrangement and I knew immediately that this was it. I just love it. You know the saying, 'Find a job you love and you'll never work the rest of your life'? Well, dear, I don't work anymore."

When you're lucky enough to do what you're "meant to do," you automatically have a career, not a job. John Stuart Mill didn't have a job *as* a reformer—he *was* a reformer. The lady at the florist shop may work at various stores over the years, and may even return to tightening bolts on car wheels, but at heart, forever, she is a florist. She'd say that the cosmos decreed this as her life's work.

I'm not so lucky, and I'd guess I'm in the majority in this regard. I haven't heard any loud, clear message from heaven announcing, "This is what you are to do with your life." Not even in a whisper. And I've been listening. So my own career, in contrast, has been a voyage adrift, as diffuse as spilled wine on a tablecloth. Other possibilities, other dreams, constantly beckon.

And, to tell the truth, for all my admiration of those with unequivocal direction, I'm not comfortable with the idea of a "calling." You've got to take a few giant narcissistic, metaphysical leaps to believe that out there in the world, waiting to be discovered, are specific occupations with each person's name attached to it. And this karmic assumption sounds less attractive when you consider that someone must have been picked to clean bedpans or to drain sewers—who wants to believe that this is his or her predetermined career? Our choice of professions isn't foreordained—we do the choosing. No doubt that decision is limited by a convergence of hereditary endowment, childhood experiences, local cultural expectations, and sheer luck. But the human species carries no gene for Web designer or talk-show host: We make the call on our calling.

Sometimes our decisions hit the bull's-eye, but sometimes they are a disaster—what sounded like a genuine calling turns out to be a ventriloquist's illusion. Here are a couple of ways many get fooled.

One siren song seduces you into unsatisfying work with the notion that you ought to do something because you're good at it. I know no better example of someone falling for this trap than Adrianne, an endocrinologist.

Adrianne is brilliant. She graduated from John Hopkins Medical School at the top of her class and now works at a top-flight hospital in Washington, D.C. She hates her job. "This isn't about the impossible demands of a research doctor's life," she explains. "The truth is, I am not that interested in medicine, particularly in the research part of it. I can get, on occasion, mildly absorbed in some new development in the field, but I'm nothing like my colleagues who get excited by conferences and journal articles. My God, they actually read this stuff for fun! I always suspected that I wasn't cut out for this specialty. It doesn't suit my personality." Why, then, I ask, did she choose this career path? "Because I was good at it, that's why," she answers. "Endocrinology is one of the more demanding areas of medicine, and relatively few women, in particular, go into the field. So I couldn't resist the temptation to do something just because it was difficult. Turns out that demonstrating how smart I was wasn't so smart after all."

The reverse mistake is to assume that even if you aren't superb at some career, you should pursue it anyway, as long as you enjoy it. "Do what you love, and the fortune will come in time," career advisers are fond of saying. Sorry for the sour note, but the real world isn't quite so accommodating. That you like what you do is a necessary but not a sufficient condition for a satisfying career. You may delight in painting fishing rods, and your designs are truly wonderful, but that is no guarantee the world will beat a path to your workshop, eager to buy your master-pieces.

Something deeper is amiss here: This is not just a mistake about the marketplace. It's a misreading of how to appreciate our lives. Many, perhaps most, of the things we do that brighten our lives can't be conscripted into a vocation; nor should they be. These interests should be celebrated, instead, for what they are . . . occasional, personally grati-fying activities.

Playing the piano is my personal example of how we lose sight of this need to protect our pleasures from our other goals. I cherish those too rare twilight hours when no one else is in the house and I have the time to sit down at the keyboard and mess about, play something cheerful or somber, as my mood mandates. I can produce a decent tune, but I'm also good enough to recognize what really good is . . . and I ain't, by a long shot. Nevertheless, when the fingers sing, I sometimes wonder with regret why I didn't choose a career in music. These are useless thoughts that only get in the way of my gratification. Why translate all our talents into potential earnings? Why can't I just enjoy my playing for what it is? Can't you revel in your gourmet cooking without operating a bistro, or delve into interior design magazines without designs on becoming a designer? In a talk about the "richness and great beauty" of the anonymous, creative life, the wise Indian thinker Krishnamurti decries this temptation to muddy our joys with dreams of extraneous reward. In *Think on These Things*, he observes:

> *Have you ever thought about it? We want to be famous as a writer, a poet, a painter, as a politician, as a singer, or what you will. Why? Because we really don't love what we are doing. If you loved to sing, or to paint or to write poems—if you really loved it—you would not be concerned with whether you are famous or not. . . . Our present education is rotten because it teaches us to love success and not what we are doing. The results have become more important than action.*

Suppose, then, that you aren't driven by a single, well-defined mission; your career could have easily taken other turns. Suppose, furthermore, that you do appreciate that some of your talents and interests cannot become the basis of your livelihood. How, then, do you decide what to do? Are you destined to flounder?

Hardly. This is the more difficult challenge, but also the more enticing one. You and I are the ones with constant options, and we have no choice but to choose. But choose on what basis?

We can agree on this. To get work done promptly, effectively, and creatively, it must be our own. Gratification comes only when the motivation is intrinsic, and both the process and the product are reflections of our own styles and values. To succeed, you really do have to like what you do.

But we would be too facile if we suggested that the type of work you do doesn't matter at all. That's not true. As Martin Luther King, Jr., reminds us, all jobs have their own potential for self-respect and sense of accomplishment, for "all work done well brings some measure of internal satisfaction." But honesty demands that we also acknowledge that not all jobs are equal. Some are the pits. Intrinsically.

The reason is neither the relative merit of the product (though that does sometimes count) nor the educational level associated with certain occupations (that doesn't count). The work of proletariat labor is vital to our communities. Until machines can take over, we need people to pick up the garbage, lay cables, and clean offices. The folks who do these chores should certainly take pride in their work. Moreover, a good argument could be made for everyone to do something like this sometime in his or her life. And yes, you can flip burgers with some degree of creativity and style. But you can't sustain this as a personal challenge year after year—there's just not enough challenge in the routine (and this, no doubt, is a problem for some investment bankers as well). You're unlikely to find satisfaction in work that is essentially repetitive and does not offer the promise of self-directed responsibilities. And you ought not to be persuaded to think otherwise by some righteous slogans.

When this becomes apparent, and you won't settle for

less, you've begun to think like an entrepreneur. Here's how it happens.

CAREER-ENTREPRENEURSHIP AND THE NEW CALLING

The artist is nothing without the gift, but the gift is nothing without the work.

—Émile Zola

Vision without action is a daydream. Action without vision is a nightmare.

—Japanese proverb

You're bored. You stare at your computer screen, wondering how many more years of this await you. You stand up and go to the window. They're putting up an awning on that new dry cleaning store across the street. "I really should start my own business," you think. Again. You've been here before more than once. Yes, "but this time I realize that the clock is running out, that at some point it becomes too late." Well, you've thought this before, too. You do have good ideas, you remind yourself. Remember how you were going to publish a newsletter for recent widows and widowers? Bet someone is already doing it. Your thoughts stroll over to the Sixties theme restaurant you once talked about opening. The best music of the era, all the waiters dressed in psychedelic clothes, the lounge set up with low couches and rugs for sitting on the floor, the smell of incense in the background. The slide show in your imagination is rudely interrupted by a phone call from reality. Someone wants to know how the memo is progressing. Your empire will have to wait.

Most people, I'd bet, have had their minutes of entrepreneurial urges. For approximately 4–5 percent of Americans each year, the itch is scratched—millions start new businesses. What distinguishes this group from the rest? Dozens of studies have tried to get a fix on the "entrepreneurial personality," but without much success. Gender, for example, is not a factor. In the primary years of entrepreneurship, ages twenty-five to forty-four, as many women open businesses as men. Wealth is not a factor either: The well-to-do and the less-than-well-to-do have about the same rate of entrepreneuring. Some personality traits certainly help. Patience, for example—it takes, on average, about twenty months before a new company is ready to do business. And ability to accept failure is surely another useful characteristic; 50 percent of all start-ups fail.

One key quality of the successful entrepreneur recognized by all is a commitment to the process, not just the result. Everyone is willing to be rich, but not everyone is willing to become rich. Entrepreneurship is about *doing*, not dreaming. This quality is crucial for the entrepreneurial career.

When people speak of entrepreneuring, they think of business, of starting a company that offers a product or service. But that's what you do. When we think of entrepreneuring, therefore, we need to broaden the scope to include not just companies but careers. Or, to express the same point differently, in the marketplace of the future, each of us is our own business. We are the entrepreneurs of our careers.

As owners of our careers, we need to underscore one vital characteristic of entrepreneurship: commitment to process. We can do what we can to assure the results we want, but there are no guarantees—too many factors are beyond are control. We are, however, in charge and responsible for the process. (Thus, Thomas Jefferson insightfully secured our right to the pursuit of happiness, not happiness itself.) The value of our work is judged not by its success in the marketplace but by the integrity with which we bring it there.

As we know too well, most of what we do never sees the light of day. Think of all those the hours spent formatting a sales report, only to have it discarded unseen because the customer decided to take his business elsewhere. And what about all those drafts of business reports that ended up in the trash bin? The effort wasted on those who weren't decision makers? So much of what we do in our work is substantial, has the legs to survive, but never goes anywhere. And when it does make it to market, it often dies there unheralded. The library has thousands of obscure books with billions of words buried inside, sitting in neglected stacks, unread, and unappreciated, perhaps forever.

All that work. But not wasted work. Not wasted, not merely because early attempts are the fertilizer of later successes, but because the endeavor itself is worthwhile. It is what we do. This commitment to the doing is truly crucial in our personal evaluation of our work and career. And it is our own appraisal that counts in the end.

From here on in, you need to sustain your career and its work. But that, in turn, requires that the work you do sustains you. It must keep you fresh, excited, and open to new opportunities. It must, in short, be creative.

The creative career

Everything that can be invented has been invented.
—Charles H. Duell,
Commissioner, U.S. Office of Patents, 1899

I haven't failed. I've just found 10,000 ways that won't work.

—Thomas Edison

Like the Holy Grail, the philosopher's stone, or the fountain of youth, human beings have been on an ongoing search for the secret of creativity. Contemporary psychologists have joined the fray, sifting through the records of the creative to find the nuggets that will reveal the keys to the treasure. They've come away with different maps.

Some say creativity is inculcated in our early lives, if not inborn. In other words, some folks got it, some folks don't. And even if all humans have some degree of creativity within them worth nurturing, our expectations should be tempered by our inherent limits. We can't all be Mozarts or Chaplins. Others see creativity as depending on serendipity and inspiration. Creative people have the special insight to recognize novelty when it comes their way. Perhaps the most often repeated story of the genre is about the inventor at the 3M company. Apparently this engineer was working on developing a strong adhesive for the company, but was only able to develop a weak one. So he redefined the problem: What is the best use of a weak adhesive? His answer was the Post-its notepaper on your desk.

The emphatic consensus of recent empirical evidence, as well as of the anecdotal reports of creative men and women, is that creativity is a function of hard work. Would-be writers and artists are always enchanted by the flashing light bulb of inspiration. They wait for the muse to grip them by the shoulder, ready to illuminate the world as soon as they have the green light. That is why they remain "would-bes." The original meaning of inspiration was "the transfusion of soul." The gods would select a deserving individual and infuse the person with a new soul. But, as Robert Grudin reminds us in his book *The Grace of Great Things: Creativity and Innovation*, the key element is the "deserving individual." Inspiration comes only to those who prepare themselves for it, for "if inspiration is indeed an enactment and transcendence, it is nonetheless impossible without groaning effort, without the painful winning of skill."

Sustained creativity, we know, requires not only a set of cognitive abilities but also a set of necessary character traits. Among them are the following:

- Passion. Only those capable of fired enthusiasm can be creative, for there is no creativity without a passion for one's work.

- Courage. It takes boldness to challenge the accepted and to risk the scorn that comes with failure.

- Humor. The humorless are too uptight to be innovative, too worried about their dignity. Creativity mandates the willingness to take a walk on the edge and risk the ridiculous.

Of all the traits that make for creative work, however, none is as essential as honesty. Intellectual truthfulness is the master virtue of the creative spirit. The journey of the creative project begins with reduction, the stripping away of the layers of presumptions that cloud vision. It begins with a return to the basics, now no longer weighed down with the accumulated baggage of limits and expectations. Free of the biases, preconceptions, and pigeonholes, you can reimagine places to go, invent new uses for your tools. The work is your creation, instilled with your integrity.

But to attain this satisfying, creative, self-motivated work, we need to get away from the notion that we are stuck at a job. We need to begin approaching our work as a self-motivated life experience, a reflection of our ourselves.

CHAPTER TWO

Making a Living or Making a Life

> *Before enlightenment*
> *chopping wood*
> *carrying water*
> *After enlightenment*
> *chopping wood*
> *carrying water*
>
> —Lao-tzu

> *If you're waiting for inspiration before you*
> *write, you're not a writer, you're a waiter.*
> —Unknown

So let's talk. It's our hypothetical scenario, so we might as well invent a comfortable setting for our discussion. We're stretched out on deck chairs on a slow-moving yacht, soaking in the rays and delighting in the soft sea breezes off the coast of the Caribbean island behind us. Out here in our idyllic sun-drenched seascape, how likely is it that that our conversation will be about work?

Not very. Maybe we'll talk of nights danced away 'till dawn in small cities with odd-sounding names. Perhaps we'll talk of our families and trace our way back to the teenage dreams we wrapped ourselves in one season and shed the next. If we talk long and openly, and the breeze turns us in that direction, we may trade war stories of the emotions, recall the times our hearts tripped with longing only to be unseemly ripped with rejection, and of the hard days of mending that followed. We'll talk about convictions come and gone, hopes victorious and hopes dashed. We'll talk about much, but not much about work. The fact is that few of us regularly associate work with the highlights of our lives.

Why is that? Why this studied neglect of 40 percent of our waking life? Compare for a moment the different ways we address love and work, life's big two needs, according to Freud. Flick on a radio station that plays songs. Any station, any type of song: top-ten now or top-ten oldies, rock hard or lite, Sinatra or Metallica, songs in English, French, or Turkish. The subject everywhere is the same: romance. Put a guitar in a person's arms, and he or she automatically turns troubadour and croons of amorous yearnings and burnings, sings tunes about getting together, being together, or breaking apart. Other than the novelty ditty or union-blues throwback, we rarely celebrate work in song.

True, we don't sing about food either—or, for that matter, about sports, platonic friendships, suntanning on yachts, politics, mutual funds, death, or all the other concentrations of our lives. I don't expect us to swing to the saga of a successful sales meeting or slow dance to the ballad of the forlorn accountant for whom the numbers never add up right. But our work lives aren't—and shouldn't be—devoid of passions worth toasting and savoring. Part of the problem may have less to with how we feel about work than with what we say about it. Part of the problem, surprising as it may seem, is that we just don't take work seriously enough.

Surprising, because on another level, we take our work very seriously. In fact, we're downright consumed with anxieties about job security and the future of our careers, with pleasing our bosses, with getting new clients while maintaining the ones we have. And aren't we all tightrope walkers dizzy from trying to balance our lives at home and at the workplace? But these concerns, immediate and important though they may be, aren't the end of the discussion. Our worries about job security and career advancement, along with the competing pressures of home and office, can be truly "solved" only if they are approached within a broader panorama, the larger scheme of our lives. We still have to get clear about how our work fits into the picture we have of ourselves.

HOW DO YOU LIKE YOUR JOB—REALLY?

A woman is badly hurt falling down the stairs and lies unconscious in the hospital for a few days. When she awakens, her doctor says, "I have good news and bad news for you. I'm sorry to tell you that your accident was quite serious. It's unlikely that you'll ever be able to work again." "And now," says the woman, "tell me the bad news."

"Do you like your job?" is a peculiar question. Sociologists have been asking Americans this for years, and the answers are consistently inconsistent.

On the one hand, people love to hate their jobs. Bumper stickers dot the highways proclaiming the drivers' distaste for work, and at the end of the week, bars everywhere invite patrons to join the TGIF party. Across cyberspace, Web sites gather people for communal bitching about their jobs. When beeped at their workplace, most people say they'd rather be doing something else. This aversion to work is not just talk. While work is not the brutal imposition of earlier years, it remains a source of major stress: More heart attacks occur at the beginning of the work week, between 8 and 9 A.M. on Monday, than at any another time. True, most people don't die to avoid work, but plenty find their jobs boring, burdensome, and pointless.

On the other hand, studies report that when asked straightforwardly whether they like their jobs, people overwhelming answer in the affirmative. In international surveys such as the Meaning of Work Project conducted in Belgium, Germany, Israel, Japan, and the Netherlands as well as the United States, approximately 80 percent of both men and women said they would continue to work even if they had enough money to live well; the more educated, the greater the percentage who'd continue to work even if money were no object. (Indeed, most people who win the lottery continue at their jobs.)

The discrepancy can be explained in part by recognizing that we sometimes have positive feelings about an activity without relishing every moment of it. You're happy that you're learning to play the cello even though you dislike practicing, and the practice takes up most of your time; even dedicated joggers are relieved when their morning run is over. So, sure, most of the time at work you can think of more fun things to do, but unless you're utterly devoid of imagination, that's probably true of 98 percent of our lives, whether we're working or not.

A more general explanation for the divergence between what we say and our genuine feelings is the streak of embarrassment we experience when we admit to liking our jobs. At the office coffee urn, it's almost natural to gripe about repulsive bosses and incompetent coworkers, and to embellish these complaints in conversations with our friends and spouses. No wonder that when we tell our children "School is your work," they echo our own expression of discontent by telling us that "School sucks."

And then, beyond the cultural norms for how we talk about work, is the nest of our own internal biases. When appraising your job, you run through a series of calculations that include the pay and work conditions, as well as such murkier factors as your level of interest, sense of accomplishment, and social relationships. The impact of all these factors is shaped by your expectations: Job satisfaction is largely determined by the match between one's expectations and actual conditions. As the research indicates, people don't so much get what they want from their careers as they learn to want what they get. This explains why older workers report more satisfaction with their jobs than younger workers—they have learned to adjust their expectations to their situations.

What molds our expectations about our jobs? One factor is the "contrast principle," developed in large part by the psychologist Harry Nelson. According to this principle, our judgments are strongly influenced by our immediate prior experiences. To test this phenomenon, here's an easy "try it yourself at home" experiment. Lift a fifty-pound weight after lifting a ten-pound weight, and then hoist the fifty-pounder after picking up a forty-five-pound weight. You'll notice that the fifty-pound weight feels much heavier after you've just lifted a much lighter weight. Psychologists observe this "relative weighing" in other spheres of our lives. A twenty-dollar payment seems like a lot more money when you previously received eight dollars for doing a job, than if the previous payment was eighteen dollars. An A on a report card feels better coming after a C than when it follows a B+. So, too, an average job will seem a lot better to you after leaving an awful one, but not so terrific after leaving a superb one.

Expectation is also influenced by anticipation. Two people have the same title in the same workplace, but one views the position as the culmination of a climb, whereas the other sees it as a springboard to higher management. Their attitudes to their jobs will differ as a result.

Adjusting your expectations about your job is a key to enjoying what you do, but be careful: Adjusting doesn't mean abandoning your aspirations. Unrealistic hope brings disappointment, but no hope brings despair. Too often, people just give up, "settle," and eventually fade into oblivion. No matter where we are in our career, we need to maintain viable plans that keep us pushing ahead to new horizons.

This is not easy, especially not for people already in, or

entering, their middle age (and their number is legion; according to census figures, for ten years beginning in January 1996, an American will turn fifty every seven and a half seconds). At this point in our lives, we grieve for the "road not taken." We're bewildered that we ended up doing what we do, and easily imagine having pursued some other profession. In our idealized counterlives, we tend to see ourselves as huge successes and ignore the inevitable tribulations that flow through even the most glamorous of careers. These unsettling emotions are further complicated by the rapid changes in the contemporary workplace. Still, we can't help but feel melancholic when we compare what is with what might have been.

Eva's mixed feelings are typical of this longing for an alternative life. She has a steady, decent sales job in the fashion industry, but her outstanding singing voice belongs to the possibilities of a different career.

Since I was a child I dreamed of being on stage—singing, dancing, acting. I still love it, and love this image of myself as performer. But I get annoyed when people tell me, "What a shame, Eva, you're so talented, you could have been a star." There must be tens of thousands of talented women out there who decided to go for it, to follow their dream. Most of them are waiting tables. I made a choice, and in the circumstances, the right one. I have a husband, three wonderful children, a decent job with some security, a different but fulfilling life. Still, I do get wistful when I visualize scenes from that "other" life. I can't help but wonder what might have been.

As we get older, many of our early options disappear for good (perhaps for bad). It's just not true that anyone can begin any new career at any point in his or her adult life. At some point we have to say good-bye to our youthful dreams and not allow them to haunt our present. We have to put those brilliant futures behind us. The tragic mistake is to turn this into the personal tragedy it is not: Other brilliant futures are still possible. Many routes of our youth are closed, but new ones are now available and promise their own rewards and surprises. This is especially true in the fluid economy of the century ahead.

The question "Do you like your job?" is, therefore, too slippery to grip with ease. We need to judge our jobs not by surface and immediate levels of contentment but in terms of how they fit in the larger trajectory of our lives. We also need to remember that our present job is not our life, nor even our career . . . it's just our current gig. We really do have choices.

FORGET BALANCE

To have a good life, you must earn a good income.
To earn a good income, you can't have a good life.
—Graffiti

Would you like a permanently thriving career and a totally fulfilling home life? Sure you would. And as long as we're sketching wish lists, why not throw a couple of million bucks into the kitty and add, say, three children, each a prodigy, each gorgeous?

We're regularly asked to compare our lives against some utopian ideal, and then wring our hands when we come up short. For example, in a 1997 survey reported in the *Wall Street Journal*, of a hundred CEOs interviewed, eighty-five said they'd like to have more time with their family, though only seven thought they'd get that discretionary time. This was presented as an eye-opening finding. But, obviously, most people who work would like to have more time with their families, just as, for that matter, most people who spend lots of time with their families would like to devote more time to their careers. In real life, people don't have enough time or energy to satisfy both their personal interests and their jobs completely. We can, however, devise a life that includes a rewarding personal life and a rewarding career.

This is where the "balance" mantra kicks in. "Achieve an even keel," we're implored, and we understand that to be a message to reduce our time at the workplace. To help nudge us in that direction, we're provided with inspirational stories of "downsizers" who have successfully split from the rat race to run a dude ranch in Montana or a bed-and-breakfast in Vermont. Somewhere in the telling, our heroes are sure to talk about "finding more balance" in their lives.

These brave souls are useful role models for the overwhelmed among us who need assurance that they'll survive a jump off the career track. Notice, though, that we rarely hear about the unfortunate renegades who didn't make it, who never got the capital they needed to operate the ranch, or had to close their charming B&B because they had no clue about how to run the place. We're warned that we work too hard, but "too hard" by whose standard? Undoubtedly, some people do spend more time at work than they should, but that hardly justifies preaching a definition of balance to which everyone must adhere.

The target of these sermons about balance is usually women. Not surprisingly. The massive entry of women into the workforce in the last quarter of the twentieth century is, unquestionably, transforming the workplace. Consider these telling figures: In 1970, thirty-two million women had jobs, a substantial 38 percent of the workforce. Twenty years later, in 1990, fifty-seven million women were working, comprising some 45 percent of the workforce. By 2005, women workers are projected to number seventy-two million, just about half the American workforce. By 1990, the "traditional" family with the father as breadwinner and the mother who stayed at home with her family accounted for less than 3 percent of American families. Even more significant, women are establishing themselves in the knowledge sectors of the workforce. In 1960, women were 4 percent of the lawyers, a mere 7 percent by 1975, up to 20 percent by 1988, and by 1997, according to the National Center for Educational Statistics, women earned 43 percent of all law degrees! In 1997, women received 37 percent of all the MBAs awarded and 38 percent of all the medical degrees. As women settle into the nation's offices and medical centers, they bring a new set of expectations about the role of the job in one's life.

For decades, a debate has raged over this development. Each side shows up armed with supporting statistics and hidden agendas: "The kids are suffering, and the moms are stressed-out," one side concludes. "Not so," says the other, "working mothers are consistently found to be far happier than unemployed mothers." We needn't revisit the details of this dispute—most people already have their mind made up. But it does come down to this: Women were criticized for staying at home and not working; then they were criticized for working and not staying at home; and now they are attacked for not doing both with appropriate balance. They can't win.

For better or worse, it seems clear that women are increasingly finding the workplace a source of satisfaction in their lives. According to the Bureau of Labor's survey, eight out of ten working women said they liked or loved their jobs. That's both true and worrisome, argues Arlie Hochschild in her bestselling book *The Time Bind: When Work Becomes Home and Home Becomes Work*. Hochschild found that Americans, women as well as men, are "making a home out of work and a workplace out of home"; they refuse flextime options and don't use all the vacation time allotted to them. Indeed, women are more inclined to spend their free time at work than are men. Why? Because, Hochschild suggests, women find more respect at work than at home, more room to be creative and to exercise their talents, more opportunity for pleasant social networking and solace in the company of coworkers. Home, on the other hand, has become more and more like work of old—an environment where efficient management, not relaxation and fulfillment, is the reigning mood. Of the people Hochschild interviewed, 86 percent thought they do a good job at work, but only 59 percent felt that way about their performance at home.

But broad generalizations about the need for more balance aren't, in most cases, relevant to the individual's decision-making process. For example, I recently noted the results of a survey in a popular magazine indicating that 48 percent of women say they are happy working even with infants at home, and 37 percent say they are very unhappy. How is a statistic like that helpful to a new mother trying to decide whether to return to her job? Typically, these articles end with an appeal for more balance. But who is to say that a quest for balance should be the central driving force at this point in *your* life?

Try giving the "more balance in your life" argument to Picasso. I bet a few of his wives tried. "Honey, you need a break. Why not put away those brushes, and we'll spend a few days in Miami? We'll relax on the beach, play a few games of pinochle, and visit with my Uncle Fred a little. Pablo, you need more balance in your life." For Picasso, life was work, work, and more work—that may account for his having produced a dozen pieces of art a day. He explained to an interviewer who marveled at his prodigious work schedule: "The passions that motivate you may change, but it is your work in life that is the ultimate seduction." Work, not balance, is the temptress of productive people. When Isaac Asimov, the science fiction writer and author of more than a thousand books, was asked what he would do if told he had only six months to live, he answered, "I'd type faster."

Let's not ignore the other pole of the yes work/no work spectrum. Some folks find no joy whatsoever in labor. They share no urgent drive to be creative and have no particular interest in being productive. They delight, rather, in gazing across blue lagoons and sipping coffee with friends in small cafés. Talk of balance entices them no more than it does the driven artist and fast-paced executive.

Most of us live somewhere between the two extremes of the fervent artist and committed layabout. We are neither monomaniacal about our work nor eager to divest ourselves of it entirely. But sometimes in our lives, our passions—directed either to our work or to our personal relationships—disturb the calming equilibrium. There is no ready formula for balance that applies throughout our lives. Nor should we allow such an assumption to shut down those driven days that so enrich our lives, in whatever sector we live it. Recognize that compromise is often the enemy of passion, and a second-rate career decision. When choosing between independence and security, says Timothy Butler, an expert on career development at the Harvard Business School, we often adopt halfway positions and end up with neither. Jumping from pole to pole isn't a wise decision either. Your most practical move, he says in an interview published in the magazine *Fast Company*, is often the one that calls for total commitment.

The most interesting moral dilemmas are not those that pit good against evil; those issues are usually easy to decide. The more difficult problems pose evil against evil or good against good. For most people, both time at work and time away from work are sources of deep gratification. That we manage to do both, even fairly well, is grounds for celebration, not sermons. Certainly, we sometimes find it hard to decide which part of our lives deserves more attention. Good versus good is always a tough decision. But making tough decisions of this kind is an indication of strength, not weakness.

One last thought about balance: Allow that people have different aspirations. One person's balance is another's obsession. Sure, the way you allocate your energies may be out of kilter and harmful; but this is the sort of determination you'll make all your life, and it depends on your current situation. "Balance" is not always the appropriate ideal. In an article entitled "Work and the Moral Woman" in the *American Prospect*, social theorist Deborah Stone reviews a spate of books on women in the workforce, and sees as the "overarching lesson" the fact that women are still subject to conflicting moral demands. She concludes that in addition to advocating changes in government and corporate policies, "We also ought to work on providing a big cultural tent in which it's possible to be a good woman and a good worker. Maybe we can accept that different women have different needs and different goals, and aim all prescriptions and policies at helping them figure out how to live well by their own moral lights."

Amen. But don't forget to do the same for us guys.

INTEGRITY AT WORK, INTEGRITY AT LIFE

My friend Paul has a problem with cigarettes. Paul is an intellectual property lawyer, and the Phillip Morris Company, manufacturer of Marlboro and other leading cigarette brands, is one of his clients. Paul has managed to overcome his misgivings about the work he does for PM, but not without strain. "Believe me," he says, "I know the rationalizations. I repeat them to myself all the time: that I work for one of the company's food subsidiaries, not the cigarette side; that all those politically correct magazines have no compunctions about advertising the product; that any enterprise whose business is legal deserves legal protection, including huge corporations that manufacture distasteful products." He adds that surely, by now, "smoking is an informed choice, not coerced." So why the discomfort, Paul? "Because at the end of the day, I have to ask myself: 'Why am I contributing my brains and time to help a company whose main product causes death?'"

This is not the internal interrogation of a self-righteous ideologue playing at sainthood. Paul is a fervent capitalist with a decidedly conservative political bent. But he values his work and therefore wants it to have value. It's important to him that what he does is part of some system that makes a positive contribution to this world.

I appreciate Paul's struggle, his willingness to confront the ramifications of his work. For the same reason, I can applaud Ellen Merlo's insistence, recounted in a *Washington Post* article, that employees at Phillip Morris have "strong values." Merlo has been with the company for nearly three decades and is in charge of its lobbying and public relations. Prospective employees who brag in the interview that they can market anything give the wrong explanation of why they would be comfortable at the company, she says, "because it shows that they really weren't thinking about the issue." The key issue, she believes, is freedom: "You don't have to believe in smoking . . . but you do have to believe in your soul that this is a choice people are entitled to make."

The ethical issues orbiting cigarettes are a stark example of how people can arrive at opposing conclusions about the integrity of their careers. Much depends on how we describe what we do—to ourselves as well as to others. In the case of smoking, for example, we distinguish between those who make the cigarettes, market them, sell them at the local store, sweep the floors at the production facility, and accept the corporation's donation to their election campaign. Of course, if you draw the circle wide enough, all human behavior is interconnected, and everything you do has moral implications—selling shoelaces in Cleveland is part of a commercial network that eventually links to the amount of grain available to feed the hungry in Somalia.

Clearly, we need to draw distinctions. Sometimes the purposefulness of your work is right there, front and center. Researchers who sacrifice big salaries to search for a cure for cancer can legitimately feel noble about their labors. On the other hand, if the guy in the gun-smuggling-for-terrorists business has no qualms about his trade, well, he ought to. Most of us, though, work in relatively neutral territory, providing goods and services that are more or less useful to humanity. We are the ones who must explain to ourselves how our work fits into the big picture and whether that picture is one in which we can take pride. Seeing your life's work from this more distant perspective is crucial.

FOR WHOM DO YOU WORK?

Humans are explaining creatures. We describe events by reference to causes and effects, through metaphors and shared conceptual frameworks. Sometimes this language enriches our explanations; sometimes it distorts it. Unfortunately, distortion is more often the rule when it comes to the descriptions of our work. We routinely repeat untested clichés and assume the truth of faded stereotypes. The consequences of these lazy linguistic habits are critical, for how we think about what we do goes a long way in determining the satisfaction we derive from what we do. It is imperative, therefore, that we recognize when we are slipping into these prepackaged models of work, presumptions that prevent us from developing a fresh vision of our careers.

Avoiding the clichés of language and judgment

Every time I teach a class on business ethics, I'm sure to have at least one smart aleck in the room who is eager to set us all straight. We're discussing, say, the issue of whistle-blowing, when and how workers should complain if their employers engage in illegal or unethical practices. This student thinks we've got it all wrong. "Businesses swim in shark-infested waters," he informs us. "You're either loyal to the captain or should abandon the ship." A contest of metaphors takes over the room. "Business is war," says one student, "and at the end of the battle, the field is left with victors and victims." "It's a jungle," suggests another, adding a complicated story about evolution and business. "I think of it rather as a game of football," still another says, "with ploys, traps, winners, and losers." But a section of the class dislikes these competitive analogues. "We need to think of business as a learning organization," someone recommends, advancing a current popular organizational theory. I also hear my share of spiritual metaphors, such as that we ought to tend more closely to the "soul of business." One metaphor after another.

In fact, however, businesses, careers, and work are what they are, not something else. Metaphors are powerful conceptual tools, and the ones we use to describe the workplace set up the framework for how we judge our lives. If you see industry as a giant machine, then it's natural to see your own work as a cog in that machine, and yourself as a replaceable part. If you describe business "as just a game," then what you do doesn't have serious consequences. When you view the marketplace as a jungle, you're bound to see its inhabitants as either predators or prey. To be sure, analogies can simplify the complex task of interpreting our occupations, but most of these comparisons have weak applications in the new workplace. Don't confuse the metaphor with the real thing.

Along with these misconstrued metaphors, our perception of work and career is clouded by stereotypical thinking about the marketplace. It is often said, for example, that the fuel of the business world is self-interest. In other words, everyone is selfish. Now, in fact, "selfish," is not another word for self-interest; the two traits are quite different. My son is acting in his self-interest when he asks me for his allowance, but he acts selfishly when he takes his sister's allowance. A robust sense of the interests of your "self" includes the interests of those you care about and those with whom you have daily commerce. The selfish, on the other hand, care not at all about the welfare of other people. You certainly can value your work for self-interested reasons—indeed, that might be the only way to value it—but the small-mindedness of selfishness inevitably collides with integrity.

Or take the related and also commonplace notion that all business decisions are based on the profit motive. In fact, profits are not the goal of an enterprise, but the means that allows an enterprise to continue to do business. That is, the point of profit is to promote business, not the other way around. The profit motive is no more a universal motive than is a "wage motive" or an "interest motive"— they all depend on features of a certain kind of economy. Indeed, management theorist Peter Drucker doubts that there is such a thing as a profit motive at all. This is an important lesson to bear in mind as we begin the new entrepreneurial career. The financial and status rewards we reap are not the aims of our careers, but tools that allow us to develop our careers still further. We will have to sell ourselves, but be careful not to sell ourselves short.

Be careful, too, of professional stereotyping: "Real estate people are lowlifes." "The television trade is run by whores." "The music industry attracts unprincipled schemers the way garbage attracts flies." "When you shake hands with someone over a deal in the fashion industry, you better count your fingers." "Lawyers . . . well, what can you expect from lawyers?"

It seems that nearly everyone thinks the business they're in is overrun by individuals with the ethics of swine—if not outright thieves, then nasty, selfish, unoriginal connivers. No doubt, some forms of commerce are rotten through and through, and appeal to people attracted to the rot. But too often, people blame a whole industry to excuse their own questionable doings. It's a lame excuse. In truth, and with few exceptions, the best in every profession and business attained their status through honorable work, not chicanery. The top lawyers, to take a much-maligned example, really do believe in the ideals of justice and professional responsibility. Respected graphic designers reject easy jobs that don't meet their high standards. Successful deal makers don't want to crush the other side, but prefer to have everyone leave the table feeling like winners.

The fellow who says "I admit my dealings are sometimes illicit, but you have to push the envelope to survive in this business," still has some growing up to do. Blaming your unethical activities on your job description doesn't cut it either— "I was only doing my duty" is the most discredited phrase of the twentieth century. In the unlikely circumstance that it is impossible for you to do your work and maintain your integrity, choose another line of work. This isn't to pontificate, but merely to remind us that our work determines how we spend most of our hours in our one-and-only lives, and it can't feel comfortable if we've spent our days concocting sordid dealings and engaging in unethical practices.

Without excuses, and willing to judge our work independent of easy assumptions, we are on the way to integrating our careers with our lives. We can, that is, reach for genuine integrity. And as part of that progress, we will have to rethink the ownership of our careers.

Reconsider your loyalties

I believe in justice, but I will defend my mother before justice.

—Albert Camus

"They have no sense of gratitude," a man says to me. "I had a fellow working here ten years. I literally took him off the streets. No experience, nothing. I brought him in anyway, gave him a job, taught him everything. Last week, he tells me he's leaving, got a better offer from the competition. We're right in the middle of our busiest season. He doesn't care. Ten years, but what does he care? 'You gotta look out for yourself,' he says to me. No gratitude, no loyalty. Nothing. That's the way it is now."

A different conversation, same argument, opposite vantage point. "Companies couldn't care less," a woman says to me. "I've worked for this company fifteen years, and gave, believe me, beyond the call of duty. I don't even want to think about those nights I stayed at my desk, working overtime for no money, because we had to get a report done before the deadline. Now my new boss calls me in—the guy has been here all of a year—and tells me that we have this impending merger and we have to cut staff. Sorry, you're gone. A polite kick in the ass and out the door. So much for gratitude."

Usually the disappearance of loyalty is expressed as a lament: Companies no longer feel any obligation to the employees and downsize them at the drop of a bottom line, while employees, for their part, will soak a company for what it's worth, then leave in a flash when it serves their purpose. This lack of mutual obligation is, supposedly, yet another indication of how basic values of the workplace have eroded.

I'm not so sure. The new understanding in the workplace has its upsides as well.

Let's reconsider why loyalty is a virtue. In his article "On Loyalty" in *The Wilson Quarterly*, political theorist Alan Wolfe offers a plausible answer. In honoring loyalty, he says, "We establish that we recognize that there is something more than our immediate instincts and desires. It forces us to confront, not flee, from our problems." Loyalty keeps us bound. It's the proving ground of our commitment. But how does this commitment play out in the contemporary work environment? What commitment are we asked to prove? And to whom—our employers? Our personal goals?

"Sex, not marriage, is the new relationship between employers and employees." Business professors Phillip Mirvis and Douglas Hall acknowledge the reality behind this description. They note in "Psychological Success and the Boundaryless Career" in the *Journal of Organizational Behavior* that "companies no longer offer their employees a commitment of 'until death do us part' and they don't expect it in return." The contemporary deal is based on mutual consent, and the terms can be anything from a one-night stand, to group participation, to fairly long-lasting serial monogamy—always with the option of altering the arrangement as expectations change.

The United States (alone in the industrialized world) sanctions "employment at will," a rule stipulating that an employee can quit without reason and an employer can fire without reason. Certain unionized groups are exempt, but this clause applies to more than sixty million workers, of whom more than two million are fired each year, hundreds of thousands of them for no cause. The contract trumps the appeal to loyalty. This new relationship is certainly not standard everywhere. For example, in the Netherlands, as elsewhere in Europe, it is illegal for either party in an employment relationship to terminate the relationship without cause, and workers can be sent to jail for trying to do so. But the trend in most modern economies is away from the traditional "relational contract" with its implied loyalty and career rewards for seniority, and toward the time-bound "transactional contract" that offers payment for specific services rendered. By 1990, 10 percent of American corporate workers were hired as independent contractors, and by century's end that percentage was close to 35 percent.

Robert Slater, in his book *Get Better or Get Beaten!*, quotes James Welch, the CEO of General Electric Corporation, as insisting that this form of association is integral to the development of the company of the future, "where we knock down the walls that separate us from each other on the inside, and from our key constituencies on the outside." This "boundaryless organization," Welch suggests, "will ignore or erase group labels such as 'management,' 'salaried' or 'hourly', which get in the way of people working together." Welch says that he now offers his personnel only a "one-day contract." (Though you can't help but notice that Welsh held on to his job for decades.)

The pioneers of this emerging work relationship are the young industries, such as health care, entertainment, and technology, that are inherently project-driven, and not weighed down by the luggage of past worker-employer expectations. In Silicon Valley, the pastoral northern California home base of the computer industry, the boundaryless organization is the reigning standard. William Hewlett, cofounder of Hewlett Packard, is reported to put it on the line to newcomers to the area this way: "If you want to succeed here, you need to do three things: change jobs often, talk to your competitors, and take risks even if it means failure."

At Microsoft, workers do not have regular hours. The

building is open twenty-four hours a day, and they can work anytime or all the time; they are accountable to their project teams rather than to individual bosses. A human resource manager at the company says executives there appreciate that "Employees drive their own development. If people want to change functions or they want to get different experiences, that's not frowned on at all." Echoing that sentiment, the program director at the Action Career Center in Cupertino, California, home of Apple Computer, concludes that "No one really expects a software developer to stay at one job for more than a couple of years here." In fact, in her experience, people who have had more jobs are generally more sought after than those who have worked for many years at the same place.

This new employer-employee compact demands a change in how you describe your profession. When asked what they do for a living, people will no longer answer "I'm with General Motors" but will say, "I'm a software engineer." Moving from job to job, continual change is integral to our "dejobbed" working lives. And people seem to be getting the message: According to a poll conducted by Towers Perin, fewer than half of the employees surveyed expected to retire from their current employer.

In the modern global economy, employer-employee relationships are, accordingly, no more than contractual. The paternalistic vestiges of the feudal company are fading—employees are neither the company's vassals nor their children, and owe no lifelong fealty to the masters/corporation. Companies now learn that they can't buy that allegiance with money either. Conversely, workers can't expect paternal security. The corporation buys abilities but need not hold our hands when we cease to service its needs.

So don't be fooled by the executive's speech about how we in the company are all a family. Families are permanent; your job is temporary. Families look out for you whether or not you deserve their care; not so your employer. Family attachment is natural; work attachments are reciprocal agreements. And even dysfunctional families respect privacy—many companies don't. According to a 1997 report from the American Management Association, a substantial percentage of companies regularly tape their employees' phone conversations, review their computer files, monitor their E-mail and videotape performance—all without the knowledge of the employees. So when you volunteer to go to the office on a Saturday afternoon, go because you're a professional, not because you're buying protection against being fired. That guarantee is not for sale.

For better or worse, we no longer take our institutions for granted. We see them as just-in-time constructions with a fleeting life span that matches the spin of our modern economy. The fading of loyalty is, therefore, not peculiar to the workplace. It has evaporated in sports, in the university, in government. But the virtue of loyalty has not disappeared . . . it has been rerouted.

In the twenty-first century, with each of us a career-entrepreneur, each of us responsible for his and her own work, we will be, as are all entrepreneurs, disloyal in our essence. Those who seek to create something new must be disloyal to the past and the status quo. Though respectful of what came before, we must refuse to see ourselves as beholden to "the old way of doing things" just because that's the way it has always been done. From here on, our strongest devotion is not to the company that hires our abilities but to our abilities themselves. Our loyalties will now be directed to the quality of our endeavors and to the workplace that honors those endeavors and encourages them.

This loyalty to our own vision can help prevent us from thinking of the entrepreneurial career as just a fancy way to refer to temporary work.

You are permanent, not a temp

When people read about the fading of permanent jobs, they think of temporary jobs as the natural alternative. According to a survey conducted by the National Association of Temporary Staffing Services, three-quarters of the respondents said they became temps as a way to look for a full-time position, and the Bureau of Labor Statistics indicates that 60 percent of people in the "contingent work force" would rather have full-time jobs.

You might be tempted to think this way, too. But as with so many other of life's enticements, make sure this is but a "temp temptation" that you manage to resist. You should feel comfortable, instead, with the 40 percent of the respondents who recognize that now all their employment contracts are transitory. Describing what you do as "just temporary," a pause in your career until a permanent job comes your way, is a last-ditch refusal to accept that everlasting employment is a relic of the past.

In fact, the incredible boom in temporary work is a vivid demonstration of how employment is changing. In the years of massive layoffs in the United States between 1991 and 1996, the number of temporary workers soared from about a million to more than 2.5 million, about 5 percent of the workforce. In the decade from 1987 to 1997, the number of people working for temporary employment agencies rose 240 percent; according to some government estimates, as of 1995, 38 percent of the labor force, some thirty-five million people, worked part-time as temps, or as contract workers. In 1997, there were between five thousand and six thousand temporary employment agencies in the Unites States, twice the number of a decade before. One of those agencies, Manpower, has 560,000 people on its roster, compared with 365,000 people who work for General Motors; based on W-2 forms issued, that makes Manpower the largest employer in the country.

These agencies are definitely finding placements for their clients—90 percent of employers use temps, and the fastest-growing segment in this market consists of skilled technicians, professionals, and even corporate executives. Corporations have strong incentives to hire temporary employees: They cost less (no benefits and pension expenditures); they have lower administrative costs; they can be hired as needed; they are more willing to do jobs full-timers won't do; and they can avoid the net of labor laws. As a result, the duration of temp employment is getting longer. For example, of the five thousand temps working at Microsoft, fifteen hundred have been there for more than a year, and some of these individuals, stringing together three-month gigs, have worked at the company for more than five years. Indeed, as the IRS will unhappily acknowledge, the distinction between permanent and temporary employment is increasingly blurred. And temps often receive decent wages—in fact, white-collar temps earn more than their permanent counterparts.

So what's so bad about life as a temp? The answer is that one crucial aspect hasn't changed: Temps are still perceived as second-class workers. Those with permanent jobs still see you as just another body passing through, transitory, uncommitted, perhaps even preventing someone more serious from getting a full-time job. Temps are rarely invited into their work community. Company managers consider them a pain to train but cheap replacement labor.

The root problem, however, isn't lower status or lack of benefits, but your self-definition. You are not a temp waiting for a real career, because you are already in the middle of your career. In our economy, jobs are activities, not positions; only the temporary contract is permanent. As I've been suggesting throughout this chapter, you, and no one else, are in charge of your career. And that is where your loyalties lie.

This new loyalty belongs to our new understanding of career and the global economy in which career will flourish. How well we succeed in this new environment will depend on our attitude to our jobs, how much of this attitude is under our control, how we spend our physical and psychic energies, and how we maintain and compromise our ethical standards in our work. We will need to commit ourselves to a personal integrity that encompasses work, leisure, and our personal relationships, that honors our abilities and our resolve to nourish those qualities. Success will also require a capacity for intense and ongoing motivation to do one's best in this uncharted frontier.

CHAPTER THREE

Motivating Your Entrepreneurial Career

THE FIRE IN THE BELLY: A PARABLE

A young aspiring violinist manages to get an audition with the great master. He takes out his violin and plays for an hour. At the end of the session, the master says to the young man, "I'm sorry, but I suggest you choose some other career. Your technical skills are fine, but you lack the essential fire in the belly." Disheartened the young man gives up on becoming a professional musician and instead goes to medical school. He does well there and goes on to have a prosperous and fulfilling career in medicine.

Our story picks up twenty years later at a party when our successful doctor again meets the great violinist, now old but still vibrant. He reminds him that they had met many years before when he auditioned for the master. "I've always meant to ask you. You suggested that I should not pursue a career as a violinist because I didn't have the fire in the belly. How did you know?"

"I didn't," the maestro answers. "I say that every time anyone auditions for me."

"But how could you?" The doctor is flabbergasted. "Suppose it wasn't me, but a future Jascha Heifetz or Itzhak Perlman or some new great talent you'd be discouraging?"

"You don't understand," explains the master. "When they have the fire in their belly, they don't care what I say."

GETTING MOTIVATED AND STAYING MOTIVATED

How do you motivate behavior? You don't.
　　　　　　　　　—Douglas McGregor, management guru

Damned alarm clock!

You're exhausted. Your eyes still shut, you reach sufficient consciousness to begin hurling blistering beads of epithets at yourself—"dimwit idiot" is the mildest. What the hell were you doing staying up so late last night? Nothing, of course. Just wasting time. Look, you blew it back when you managed to be born to parents not able to provide you with independent wealth so you'd be spared this enslavement to a heartless clock with its unrelenting, monomaniacal "Time to get up, time to get up." Well, guess what? It's time to get to up and go to work. Damn!

So you saunter through the morning rituals and you're almost awake by the time you walk out the door, into the world, and off to your job. Why do you bother? Why do you go to this job every day?

Yes, I do understand: A body demands its food and a landlord his rent. But I'm also aware that money can't be the whole story. You could make your living lots of ways, and with some planning and a few years of training, you'd bring home an even larger salary doing something other than what you do now. It's not income alone luring the CEO to his office at seven-thirty every morning and keeping him there until ten in the evening. It's probably not just the money that draws you to your work, either.

The great ones, those who make the big contributions to their field, never do it solely for the bank account. Jonas Salk didn't spend years searching for a cure for polio because he wanted more discretionary dollars: "I feel that the greatest reward for doing is the opportunity to do more," he said. Van Gogh didn't bring his swirling visions to the canvas because he espied a marketplace of eager buyers—in fact, the poor guy didn't sell a single painting in his entire life. So, too, Galileo, Whitman, Houdini, Fellini, Puccini, and every other master in every field of human enterprise were not, and are not, driven in the main by power, wealth, fame, or other external satisfaction. This list includes the entrepreneurial titans of capitalism, too, for whom making money is never just about making money. What they share is a more powerful motivation: the work itself.

When the pioneers talk about incentive, they always refer to the determination to exceed the limits, to defy the presumptions. Einstein couldn't be restrained by the humdrum goal of becoming "the world's best physicist"—he was too busy trying to figure out how the universe worked. Michael Jordan, no doubt, found the personal glory delicious, but what kept him pushing his talent was the passion to play basketball as no one imagined the game could be played. This dedication is not, however, just the preserve of superstars—you hear the same resolve from the fulfilled social worker, the innovative marketer, the creative designer, the stalwart surgeon, the inspiring teacher, and the efficient secretary. People who drive around with bumper stickers that say "Work sucks" or "I owe, I owe, it's off to work I go" are not the people who excel at what they do.

You already know this. When the work goes well, and you're "in a zone," too engrossed to notice the clock or think about the money and recognition, when you're too absorbed even to notice that you are absorbed—at moments like these, lost in your work, you find yourself. True, these experiences are too infrequent, but having had them, we recognize what genuine motivation tastes like. The rest of the time, we settle for mundane rewards to keep us energized. But it isn't the same, and our work pays the price in joy and creativity.

We're too cynical these days to talk about internal satisfaction of work without embarrassment. And it's difficult to get an unobstructed view of when our work truly gratifies without first scraping away all the tacked-on goodies that clutter our lives. Let me assure you that this discussion is not a sly segue into a sermon about the purity of work and the evils of selling ourselves to ephemeral temptations. The questions here are straightforward and practical: Why is discipline such an issue in your life? Is it something about you, the work you do, or perhaps an incompatibility between the two? What makes some of your work time glide, as opposed to the rest of the time, when it just plods along? The answer to all of these questions centers around your attitude to what you do. To dig deeper here, we need to take a brief expedition into the psychology of motivation.

THE PRICE OF THE PRIZE

The first visit to one of the new massive casinos is always astonishing. The otherworldliness of the place. The constant noise. You're startled at the sight of all these people, mostly women, mostly older, seated in neat rows, zealously dropping chips into slot machines. Periodically, above the din, you hear the ringing bells announce the visit of Lady Luck, followed by a delighted shriek of "Yes, finally!" as chips tumble into an eager hand cramped from waiting so long for this small affirmation. Win or lose, the parade of quarters steadily marches into the machine, one after the other, hour after hour, all day, any day. And all evening, any evening, in quiet offices high above the action, casino owners count the day's take and offer thanks to their investors and the enduring laws of probability.

They should also be grateful to B. F. Skinner and his pigeons.

Do you remember classical conditioning from your introductory class in psychology? The basic idea, you'll recall, is that if every time you do something, something else happens, eventually you begin to associate the second event with the first. For example, this discussion of behaviorism might trigger thoughts of Pavlov's dog, the famous mutt of conditioning theory: You ring a bell and bring Spot his food, keep doing that, and before long the mere sound of the bell gets old Spot to salivate. B. F. Skinner improved on this model by introducing the notion of operant conditioning. He demonstrated that not only a prior stimulus but also a later stimulus conditions behavior, or in the theory's lingo, we positively reinforce behavior by rewarding it and negatively reinforce behavior by punishing it. Spot pees on the carpet, you smack him with a rolled-up newspaper, and sure enough, soon enough, Spot no longer confuses the living room with the street. Experimental psychologists spent the next decades investigating which had the greater impact, the carrot or the stick, positive reinforcement or negative reinforcement. They also designed optimum schedules of reinforcement—how often you needed to provide the lollipops or administer the shocks to make or break a habit.

And this brings us to Skinner's pigeons, the one-armed bandits of the gambling temples, and the stack of memos on your desk awaiting your attention.

Casinos can't remain in business if patrons score every time they pull the lever; on the other hand, if the gamblers never hit the jackpot, they'll soon gather their quarters and go back to their bingo cards. (Lotteries are able to attract bettors by offering fairy-tale payoffs.) The challenge to the gambling establishment, therefore, is to fix the odds so that the urge to bet remains intense, although at the day's end most of the customers' cash will end up in the owners' pockets.

Pigeons to the rescue. People, it turns out, are similar to animals when it comes to simple stimuli responses—the optimum rate at which gamblers will play slot machines is strikingly akin to the optimum rate pigeons will peck a lever to get food. And in like manner, the celebratory chimes accompanying the infrequent win add a bit of reinforcing champagne to the habit.

This bare model of motivation may explain pigeons' pecking behavior, humans' slot machine addiction, and perhaps the success rate of behavior modification therapists using threats and bonuses to eliminate phobias and compulsive behaviors such as smoking. But in recent years, psychologists have recognized that Skinnerian behaviorism, although far more sophisticated than the sketch of the theory drawn above, can't explain the more complex aspects of people's beliefs and behavior; you can't easily extrapolate from the zigzag of a rat in a maze to Rembrandt deciding on a hue of blue for his painting.

The appeal of behaviorist thinking runs deep and isn't easy to dislodge. Most of us are convinced that rewards are the best way to motivate people. A serious problem with this approach is that, in general, it isn't true. In fact, punishments and rewards sometimes have the opposite effect of what was intended.

HOW REWARDS PUNISH

Do rewards motivate people? Absolutely. They motivate people to get rewards.

—Alfie Kohn

Then Speaker of the House Newt Gingrich congratulated West Georgia College for paying third graders two dollars for each book they read. Said Gingrich, "Adults are motivated by money—why not kids?"

A linchpin of behaviorism collapsed when researchers observed that even when conditioning works, it usually doesn't work for long. Remove the reward or punishment, and the motivation disappears, too.

Robert Deci demonstrated this phenomenon in a seminal experiment he conducted in the 1970s. Deci gave two groups of people a fun puzzle to play with called Soma. He paid the first group for their participation, but not the second group. He noticed that when the experimenter was out of the room, those in the nonpaid group were much more inclined to fiddle with the puzzle than those in the compensated group. And when the participants believed they were involved in a competition, both those who won and those who lost were comparatively uninterested in playing with the puzzle after the experiment was over and their performance no longer counted. Further studies by Deci and others confirmed that the desire to do something for the sake of doing it has greater staying power than the desire to do it because of some other benefit or the fear of the repercussions for not doing it.

We are averse to accepting this finding. We just assume—and the assumption runs extremely deep—that rewards are what motivate us to do well. We learn to believe this early on—the appeal of rewards as the chief means of encouragement is a fixture in our schools. In kindergarten, we flood our children with stickers, stars, certificates, and trophies, oblivious to the dangers of setting up awards as educational goals.

Here's a telling, recent example. Community leaders in a Midwestern town, upset about the lack of interest in reading among schoolchildren, came up with the bright idea of offering a free pizza to any child who read ten books or more within a specified period. Several kids did win the free pizza, but they read only the ten slimmest, easiest books they could find. More insidiously, this scheme intensified these children's disdain for reading. When you reward someone with Y for doing X, you implicitly indicate that you value Y more than X. Tom Sawyer had that figured out when he had his friends pay for the privilege of painting his fence. This is why, when you give a child a felt tip pen and tell him that if he agrees to use the pen, he will get a crayon later, the child will value the crayon over the pen; do the reverse, and the child will value the felt tip pen over the crayon. Those town officials would have done more for their literary cause had they offered a free book to any child who ate ten pizzas.

The appeal of offering rewards to get people to do what

you want is entrenched in managerial thinking, says Alfie Kohn, a leading critic of compensation systems. In *Punished by Rewards*, he notes, "It takes time and effort and thought and patience and talent to solve problems and help people do their best . . . in many workplaces, incentive plans are a substitute for management." Many managers prefer to bribe employees who are underachieving than take the trouble to understand why they aren't working at capacity. One critic calls this the game show approach to management: "And now, ladies and gentleman, just by selling more widgets, you can win fabulous prizes!" But all of us, not just the managers, persist in thinking that without payment, nothing would get done: "Why bust your butt working if you don't get anything out of it?" This, of course, depends on what you mean by "don't get anything out of it." For here's the kicker: When what you get out of it is only external benefits, and not the joys of the work itself, motivation goes down, not up.

The idea that money doesn't spur productive work may sound suspiciously "feel-good" and divorced from the concrete reality of our work lives, but the hard evidence suggests that this is precisely the case. When children are remunerated for writing poetry or painting, their product is consistently judged as less creative than when they aren't compensated. Students paid to study do worse on follow-up exams than those who study because they enjoy the subject or because they've been asked to teach it to others.

So, too, in the workplace. The research shows that monetary incentives can improve performance, but only when the tasks are mindless (why else would anyone spend the

74

day licking envelopes?) or when the workers dislike what they're doing. And though productivity does surge immediately after a wage increase, the output soon returns to previous levels. In an oft-quoted article in the *Harvard Business Review*, Fred Hertzberg concludes that money doesn't motivate—the best it does is prevent you from hating your job. You'd be furious if your salary was cut by a third, but if it were raised by a third, you wouldn't love your job more than before. Hertzberg's advice to managers is "If you want people motivated to do a good job, give them a good job to do." David Hofrighter, Vice President and Managing Director of the Hay Group, a compensation consulting firm in Chicago, tells his clients: "Pay directs behavior, but motivation is strictly an inside job." Indeed, ask yourself—but not so loud that your boss overhears you—whether your work habits have significantly improved since your last raise. Probably not. Money, like a whip on the back, can get you to work, but it can't get you to want to work. Only the enterprise itself can provide that internal commitment.

The distinction between internal drive and external manipulation is especially critical in dealing with your personal discipline. For even if pay incentive schemes are effective in the workplace, they aren't an effective tool for motivating yourself. Managers are primarily interested in short-term performance, but you have to live with yourself for a long time. Each time you bribe yourself to get to work, you chip away at your self-respect. These mind games are thin devices that don't address the core question of how seriously you take yourself and your responsibilities.

Rewards are demeaning

Despite all the recent enlightened managerial rhetoric, employees are still commonly viewed as passive organisms waiting to be stimulated. As sociologist William Foote Whyte says in *Money and Motivation: An Analysis of Incentives in Industry*, "In the case of machines, management turns on the electricity. In the case of workers, money takes the place of electricity."

Dangling pay raises as rewards for quality work offends self-motivated employees because, as Alfie Kohn observes in *Punished by Rewards*, "When responsible action, the natural love of learning, and the desire to do good work are already part of who we are, then the tacit assumption to the contrary can be fairly described as dehumanizing." Having your personal intentions discounted is degrading. How would you feel if your neighbor offered to give you five dollars for your kindness in driving him to the train station, or if your spouse proposed to give you five dollars for making love to him/her?

When you encourage people by promising a reward, you treat them as evolved hamsters in an experimental maze. And just as we need to value other people's dignity, so we need to respect our own. We dishonor ourselves when we insist that only a new Jaguar and a round of applause can inspire us to take our work seriously. The car is lovely and the applause is sweet, but their appeal weakens with time. In the end, discipline is generated only by what you value about yourself. This self-discipline will be your crucial ally as you form your career in the new global workforce.

Rewards subvert relationships

Compensation-based incentives not only ignore people's self-motivation but also reinforce imbalances in power. The reward structure—"Do what I want, and I'll throw you a bone; don't do what I want, and you get nothing"—is an overt reminder of who is in charge of whom. We know firsthand the condescending flavor of favors promised and withdrawn. No wonder we sometimes have an urge to defy those who deign to reward us.

Reward systems also undercut cooperation. The teacher who awards only three honor certificates to the class sets up a contest that begets rivalry and envy. Limited rewards in the workplace, such as promotions and bonuses, transform your colleague and friend into someone standing in the way of your success. Some people relish this sort of competitiveness and are galvanized by the prospect of winning when that means others lose. But this competitive disposition is usually a barrier to excellence. More important, it leaves a sour residue on our tongues—we want to be inspired by something more enriching than the defeat of others.

You're not likely to do your best when your sole aim is to please your boss; your work will belong to him, not you. Similarly, when your prime motive is to surpass your associates, you are dependent on other people and your product is likely to be second-rate. We are at our peak only when the standards of excellence are our own.

Rewards discourage risk-taking

Rewards are the enemies of exploration. When a rat in a maze discovers a route to the food, it won't try any other path, thus ignoring possible shortcuts. People who work just for the pay also do what they must, and no more. They, too, are risk-averse, wary of untried roads, unwilling to follow hunches or rethink their goals.

Sometimes this conservatism is reasonable. When your only interest is getting paid, you carve out the easiest, quickest, surest way to finish the assignment. But what if you can do better? What if there is an even easier, more elegant way to do the job? Take note that tying the quality of your work to payment is habit-forming: Today it's this project and this boss, tomorrow it's some other job and some other compensation. It's easy to see how this pattern is a prescription for mediocrity. Weighed down by the anticipated payoff, your creativity can't sail in new directions on uncharted waters. And what a loss that is.

THE INTRINSIC JOYS OF INTRINSIC MOTIVATION

This sweeping, feverish indictment of rewards needs to be tempered. Surely, external reinforcements are sometimes appropriate—you're not going to lose interest in your work just because a client thanked you for the magnificent job you did. Moreover, some motivational theorists believe that external dividends can help jump-start projects you'd otherwise avoid, and proponents of "learned industriousness theory" assert that rewards for efforts at difficult tasks can generalize into a greater willingness to try other tough assignments.

The critical factor is how the rewards are administered. When granted as an extra plum, not as a judgment, rewards do no harm. Rewards are subversive, however, when they become the goal of your efforts or are used to control behavior. This is borne out in an intriguing study on the different ways men and women respond to praise. The men were less affected by praise, apparently because they expected the approval for their performance, while the women were more surprised by the acclaim—they turned the commendation, not just the work, into a goal in itself. Nevertheless, for both men and women, praise reduced self-motivation when it was presented in controlling terms—for example, as a mechanism to compare one's ability with that of someone else. What we need to make our work satisfying and successful is intrinsic motivation.

This is the true joy in life, the being used for a purpose recognized by yourself as a mighty one; the being a force of nature instead of a feverish, selfish little clod of ailments and grievances complaining that the world will not devote itself to making you happy.

—George Bernard Shaw

Moral philosophers draw an important distinction between instrumental goods and intrinsic goods. Instrumental goods derive their value from the benefits they bring about. A superb stereo system has instrumental merit because it provides the pleasures of listening to great music. Having your teeth cleaned by the dental hygienist is an instrumental good because, for all the annoyance associated with the visit, it beats the alternative pain of tooth decay. What are intrinsic goods, the ends-in-themselves? Happiness? Truth? Spiritual enlightenment? Beauty? A combination of these?

This complex inquiry engaged the thinking of Socrates and the philosophers who followed him for more than two thousand years. Some inclined to the view that there must be a single, overriding intrinsic value, one final good to which all others should lead. For example, one popular candidate for this final intrinsic good is hedonism, a life devoted to pleasure; in this framework, knowledge and beauty attain their value only insofar as they lead to pleasure. Other philosophers argue that we could have several different intrinsic goods, even if sometimes they might conflict with one another. A related philosophical question, one discussed at length by current philosophers, is whether each individual is the best judge of his own well-being, and that satisfying one's desires is an intrinsic good. But others insist that there is an objective judgment of well-being that we, as individuals, may get wrong. (For example, the miser spending his life holed up in his room counting his money might be fulfilling his desires, but he is not "objectively" living the best life he could.) So fulfilling your desires is no guarantee that your life goes well.

We won't resolve here what qualifies as a good-in-itself, but we should note how contemporary society systematically confuses instrumental values with intrinsic values.

On the one hand, we turn means into ends. We need to eat healthy foods in order to live, but some people live in order to eat well, worrying more about eating right than getting on with their lives. Similarly, the benefit of money is in what it can buy, but so many turn having money into the goal.

On the other hand, we regularly turn ends into means. You stand enchanted on a cliff at dusk, watching the sun fold its golden fan and cast its final glints of golden light on the rocks below, and you think, "Wow, if only I had a camera." Even our most momentous moments are experienced as material for something else. The philosopher Charles Taylor, in *The Ethics of Authenticity*, calls attention to this cultural malaise of "instrumental reasoning," where even personal relationships are approached in terms of a cost-benefit ratio.

Our attitude toward work is another example of this inversion of means and ends. Much of our labor is instrumental, bringing us the food, furniture, clothing, and vacations we crave along with the more abstract delights of admiration and status. But work is also a locus for intrinsic contentment; watch a painter "at work," a baseball pitcher in action, or a salesman on a roll. To see work as only or even primarily instrumental is to cheat oneself of one of life's most satisfying intrinsic pleasures.

When is work an intrinsic good? When *it gratifies our natural curiosity*, when *it makes demands on our talents*, when *it manifests our autonomy* and when *it provides the experience of flow*. Let's look more closely at each of these qualities.

The lure of curiosity

> *Curiosity killed the cat but for a while I was a leading suspect.*
>
> —Steven Wright

The similarity between simians and people makes us nervous. It also makes us laugh, for anxiety often translates into humor—think of the scatological jokes of children and the sexual jokes of adults. These physical affinities—humans and chimpanzees have 98 percent of their DNA in common—have been a boon to medicine, providing not only effective tests for new drugs but even organs for transplant. Investigations of simian behavior have also taught us much about our own psychological tendencies.

In one of his landmark studies of rhesus monkeys in the 1950s, Harry Harlow scattered puzzles in a cage (presumably monkey puzzles, not the Sunday crossword variety) and watched as the animals manipulated the pieces for hours at a time, for no reward other than the sheer pleasure of exploration. They were acting from what Harlow called "intrinsic motivation." Monkeys have an abiding curiosity about their environment.

Humans, too, are naturally inclined to acquire new information, absorb new ideas, try out new tools, pursue new approaches, develop new skills, and expand their skills. Stifle people's curiosity by having them repeat the same work every day, and they become unbearably restless. Exploration is its own reward.

Satisfaction of curiosity is crucial to any successful career. You have an innate need to try new paths, and your life's work should provide those new opportunities.

Making use of our talents

Human curiosity is perhaps unique in that it is directed not only to the outside world but inward as well. This interest includes our own talents and abilities. We want to know how far we can push our skills, and we seek challenges that put our faculties to the test. We want our work to make demands on us, and we grow restless when it doesn't.

Nothing is as exhausting as underachieving. When you continually work below your optimum, forced to dumb down, day in and day out, your spirit evaporates. Mere coasting is deadening, and the aphorism is right to advise us that "It is better to wear out than to rust out."

Only a few professions afford the possibility of working at capacity nearly all the time. A baseball player, for example, is welcome to hit a home run every time he gets up to bat. But even the athlete isn't expected to score on every turn. Somerset Maugham noted that "only mediocre writers always perform at their best." For the vast majority of us, the job entails stretches of tedium. An orthopedic surgeon tells me that while he might have more riveting moments at work than most people, he, too, still rues the amount of time he underperforms each day. "Much of it," he laments, "is spent filling out mind-numbing insurance forms and dealing with office management chores, not in doing anything I looked forward to in medical school."

Every job—the surgeon's, too—has its stretches of drudgery, of course, but the critical question is whether these no-brainer patches overwhelm the time when you actually get to do some innovative work. Prolonged boredom can be fatal, if not to our bodies, then surely to our careers; enthusiasm can be "bored to death." And beware: Monotony is a devious enemy. It lowers your expectations, suffocates your motivation, and then hides behind the formidable force of inertia, wreaking such havoc on our resolve that, as Nietzsche says, "Against boredom even the gods themselves struggle in vain."

To escape the stupor, we sometimes turn to stupidity. We make the desperate mistake of taking on projects that are too difficult or unwieldy. The result is boredom, once again. You concentrate on your project for a brief spell, give it an honest try, but soon your interest takes a stroll and you dissociate from the work. You can't lose yourself in tasks that are either too easy or too strenuous, and invariably the quality of your output reflects that lack of attention.

Unfortunately, the possibility of finding yourself trapped in years of numbing work is frighteningly real.

To avoid this fate, *you have to consciously carve out a career that brings you jobs complex enough to demand your best but not so complex that you will frequently fail.* Researchers in motivational psychology have found that when we work to meet "just manageable difficulties," not only do we work at our optimum, but we also feel a lot better about ourselves for making the effort.

How do you establish your level of "just manageable difficulty"? Studies suggest that motivation is at its maximum when the failure/success ratio is about 50:50. Remember, though, that levels of difficulty change as your skills improve or decline. The "gravitational hypothesis" posits that people tend to find themselves, eventually, in jobs that are compatible with their abilities. Job dissatisfaction, getting fired, or quitting, this theory suggests, can often be explained by this internal drive to gravitate to a job that has a good fit. But you can't count on this natural migration to the "right job." You might also undertake a venture beyond your ken because the returns, whether money, pride, or love, are extremely important to you. Sometimes, too, a gust of optimism convinces you that you can beat the odds; although most new businesses fail, no entrepreneur ever made it who didn't think he had that extra something going for him. These, however, are the exceptions. In general, you want to develop a career where your success depends on the intensity of your effort and intrinsic motivation keeps you pushing your talents.

Manifesting your autonomy

Work out your own salvation. Do not depend on others.
—Buddha

A favorite thought experiment of philosophy professors has become a cliché in movies about invaders from outer space. Imagine that in the course of a CAT scan, doctors discover that your brain contains hundreds of tiny computer chips implanted by inhabitants of some distant galaxy. By manipulating these chips, the aliens control all your behavior, your thoughts, even your feelings—your whole life is something like their personal Nintendo game. You're not the one who decided to go to Ireland this summer or to eat the pistachio nut on the right side of the plate. These decisions were made by an alien playing with his remote control.

Would this be devastating news? After all, you did have the experiences you think you did—those were real feelings, even if you were mistaken about their source. And why couldn't you go on living as you did before? You couldn't, because knowing that the decisions you make are not your own changes everything. You no longer can think of yourself as a self. Your very identity has been destroyed, for inherent to our concept of an adult person is responsibility for one's choices. Without autonomy, you are an automaton.

When others dangle external rewards and punishments to get us to do what they want, our autonomy is under attack. As we noted, sometimes that's acceptable. We understand why the police ticket us for speeding, and why scientists win Nobel Prizes. We also sometimes find it helpful to play these reward/punishment mind games with ourselves, too, promising ourselves little treats for our accomplishments and threatening to deprive ourselves if we screw up. But, for the most part, it is essential that we see ourselves as the originators of our actions, not a manipulated link in someone's design. Effective managers are aware that the most efficient way to get people to do what you want is to make it seem that the idea was their own.

Richard deChalmes studied the effects of autonomy on outcomes and found that people who perceive themselves as the originators of their activities are more intrinsically motivated than others. But remember that autonomy does not mean working alone or in competition with others. Indeed, cooperation, at its best, involves independent, autonomous individuals working together. Nor does autonomy preclude you from receiving benefits for your output, though the central benefit should be the fulfillment of your own interests.

There's a lesson here for all of us. We are unceasingly bombarded with "tips" on how to get things done: five steps to better dieting; the secrets of better money management, better parenting, better relationships, better everything. Assuredly, some of these techniques help. But if we ever want to own our lives and develop discipline based on internal drive, not external authority, we need to get beyond manipulating ourselves with tricks and treats; their potency soon runs out, in any case. Motivational maturity is about self-rule, taking yourself and your choices seriously.

Go with the flow

> *I want to be thoroughly used up when I die, for the harder*
> *I work, the more I live. I rejoice in life for its own sake.*
> —George Bernard Shaw

Perhaps the best way to introduce the work of Mihaly Csikszentmihalyi is by autobiographical confession. I first came across his name as I was skimming through a book on alternate states of consciousness. I also read that Csikszentmihalyi was the author of a book titled *Flow.* Flow? Pardon me, but I think I'll go back to real science.

Well, lo and behold, Mihaly Csikszentmihalyi is a scientist, and a good one. His assertions about flow may appear soft-minded with intimations of a faded hippie philosophy, but experiment and rigorous methodology support them. Moreover, what he has to say about work, leisure, and creativity is sensible and important.

Csikszentmihalyi asks you to imagine yourself skiing down a slope. Your attention is focused on the movement of your body, the position of the skis, and the air whistling past your face. You notice the snow-shrouded trees as they hurry by you. You are completely immersed in your experience and have neither time nor inclination to think about your worries—a distracting emotion might get you buried facedown in the snow. But who wants to get distracted anyway? The run feels so right. You wish it would last forever. You are in the flow.

Or observe the woman gardening in the backyard. Notice how focused she is on what she's doing. This is clearly a labor of love, not for wages. You can witness that same absorption in the person caught up in her music, in the chess player during a match, in the businessman closing a deal, in the scholar researching her text, or in the mother playing with her baby. These self-motivated activities are further examples of flow.

The distinct feeling of total immersion in one's actions has been, of course, previously noted. Zen Buddhism, for example teaches how we can become one with what we do. This experience is also a pivotal feature in the influential humanist psychology of Abraham Maslow. Unlike the behaviorists, who study laboratory rats, or Freudians, who focus on neurosis and dysfunctional human behavior, Maslow wanted to investigate what makes people excel. Basing his findings on in-depth interviews with highly productive, noteworthy individuals, he postulated a hierarchy of motivations moving up from our basic physiological needs through our desire for safety, social interaction, and self-esteem, to the highest level of motivation, which he called "self-actualization." Self-actualized people, according to Maslow, have accurate perceptions of themselves and the world, are spontaneous and creative, enjoy being alone, have few social prejudices, and are open to "peak experiences" characterized by total involvement in their work. Few people, Maslow believed, ever achieve self-actualization.

Csikszentmihalyi, on the other hand, insists that ordinary people regularly attain states of flow in the course of their ordinary work and leisure. Moreover, you can train yourself to have more flow in your life. Here are three essential elements that help create a flow experience.

1. Have clear goals. Whether you are scaling a mountain or revising a business plan, when you're in the flow, your goals are unambiguous and attainable. In addition, the feedback is immediate—you can tell right away whether or not you are getting closer to your destination.

2. Lose self-consciousness. Artists talk about "aesthetic rapture," how the muse seems to write their story or moves their brush across the canvas; mystics describe the spiritual heights of "effortless effort" and the collapse of ego in religious ecstasy (ecstasy = "to stand outside oneself"); athletes attribute an extraordinary performance to their having been "in the zone" of total focus. All these moments are akin to flow. The sense of time's passage is altered; one is "in the present" throughout. Paradoxically, because all of you is in the present, this isn't about you at all. And because your self-consciousness is on vacation, you don't get in the way of your accomplishment. Neither the judgments of others nor the promise of external benefits matters. You claim the activity as your own, and that is self-rewarding.

3. Respond to autonomy, curiosity, and challenge. The three elements of intrinsic motivation we discussed earlier are all integral to the flow experience. We are most involved when presented with novelty and the possibility of new discoveries. Flow is not a trance. We are most absorbed in what we do when our mind is active, searching for new developments, innovative strategies; you can be in the flow conducting a symphony orchestra or parking cars in a garage. To maintain this interest, the activity must challenge: it can't be too easy or too difficult. And it must be of our choosing; we are not engrossed in what we do when it is imposed on us by others. Flow requires autonomy.

These moments of flow, we need to reiterate, are not the preserve solely of the artist, mystic, or athlete. They are accessible to all of us. The first step in enhancing flow in our life is to appreciate its value. Without these periods of total engagement, our work is always work for hire. It can never be truly joyful. To achieve more flow, we need to learn how to let go and lose ourselves in our work.

We can build flow activities into the normal course of our workday and our work. We can try to invent new ways to do our mundane chores, create new challenges, new ways to communicate with customers, clients, and colleagues. We need to be realistic, too. Can you find flow in sorting the mail every day? Probably not, and that is reason enough to look at the larger picture, to make certain there are other opportunities for flow in your work life.

While flow experiences are a critical part of the intrinsic motivation to do one's work, they are not enough to guarantee a nourishing work life. After all, sadists and serial murderers, mercenary soldiers in battle, hucksters, and thieves, can all be in states of flow. True satisfaction with the flow time in our work and leisure occurs only when we *value* how our time is spent. So, too, as we shall see next, we connect with our work best when we respect what we produce and determine our own definition of success.

CHAPTER FOUR

Winning, Losing, and Knowing the Difference

Lord, grant that I may always desire more than I accomplish.

—Michelangelo

Your dreams can't come true until you first wake up.

—Anon.

MEASURING SUCCESS: AMBITION, ENVY, AND COMPETITION

The ambiguous allure of ambition

I always knew I wanted to be somebody. I realize now that I should have been more specific.

—Lily Tomlin

The desire for success lubricates secret prostitutions in the soul.

—Norman Mailer

WORK

> *The exclusive worship of the bitch-goddess Success is our national disease.*
>
> —William James

Do you wish you were more ambitious?

Most people answer with a halting "yes," the tentativeness reflecting their discomfort with their answer. We have mixed feelings about our own ambitions and a double standard when we attribute ambition to others. Listen to how Melissa describes Everett, a colleague at work.

"The guy is forever sucking up to the boss and anyone else he thinks might help his career. When an executive at a meeting suggests, 'Wouldn't it be a good idea to blah blah blah,' bet on Everett to pipe up with 'Absolutely, I think blah blah is a terrific idea, the timing is perfect, and we really ought to try it.' Count on our Boy Scout to volunteer for even the dullest committee work, provided, of course, that the right people notice his contribution. Everything he does is self-serving." Melissa's distaste for Everett's ambition drips from her every word.

Now listen to Melissa talk about herself. "I really have to start marketing myself. I'm not going anywhere in this company, and it has nothing to do with competence and everything to do with not selling myself. It's strange, but I have no problem promoting other people, yet I'm so uncomfortable when it comes to promoting myself. I wish I was more driven, but I just don't have it in me."

How genuine is Melissa's self-condemnation? Notice the subtext of her complaint (or your own complaint) about not being sufficiently ambitious, and you can detect not only self-reproach but also pride in not being pushy like some others. This brew of self-criticism and self-congratulation cuts across the professions. In the past few months I've heard it expressed by corporate executives, doctors, caterers, musicians, a magician, editors, a deli owner, a professor of marine biology. And I can't recall meeting a therapist who didn't tell me that she'd have many more clients if only she marketed her practice more aggressively, attended more professional meetings, and went to the "right" parties.

The source of this ambivalence traces to a fundamental conflict in our culture's values. On the one hand, we preach the virtue of contentment: "Be satisfied with what you have." We prize the wisdom of the Roman philosopher Epictetus when he counsels: "Do not spoil what you have by desiring what you have not, but remember that what you now have was once among the things hoped for." The rich man, we teach, is the one who is content with his possessions. This is also the central insight of Buddhism: To achieve inner peace, one must let go of one's cravings. So, too, a thousand other sages in a thousand other articulations warn that a life of constant grasping for more ... more wealth ... more honor ... more pleasure ... reflects a troubling flaw in character and is a recipe for unhappiness.

But we also preach a contradictory virtue, and with no less conviction: "Never be satisfied with yourself." We exhort people not to accept their situation but to strive for constant improvement, to do better, to recognize that "you can't steal home and keep your foot on third base," and to accept that you must take risks to move up the ladder. Indeed, some say, the key word in the Eastern call to achieve enlightenment is "achieve." According to this equally esteemed team of sages, satisfaction with one's circumstance reflects a troubling flaw in character and is a recipe for stagnation.

So what are you to do? Stop driving yourself nuts trying to get ahead and become comfortable with who you are, or refuse to rest on your fading laurels and, with your eye the next horizon, go for it? Does your aversion to other people's ambition manifest your inherent decency or your envy? All this takes sorting out.

We begin with two essential principles.

1. Ambition is a choice. Melissa says of her unwillingness to promote herself, "I just don't have it in me," as if ambition were a bug that runs in your bloodstream, a quality like a good singing voice or a fast metabolism that's inbred in your genes or bred into your upbringing, something over which we have no control. Nonsense. Ambition results from how you choose to see yourself in the world. Don't blame it on your DNA.

2. Ambition aims at specific targets. The wise guy says, "I don't know what I want, but I want it now," but in fact there is no ambition "in general." Every ambition has an objective such as wealth, power, or affection. Eric's ambition is to make it to retirement, get his pension, and move to Wyoming for a quiet life of reading and fly fishing. Kim intends to make her way to the top of the corporate ladder and work until the day she dies. Don't ask yourself vague, imprecise, and distracting questions such as "Should I be more ambitious?" Ambition is deciding where you want to go and what you're prepared to do to get there.

It may be of some comfort to know that few people actually choose their own goals. Most have only the vaguest sense of what they consider a successful career for themselves, and an even murkier notion of what they'd count as a failure. Instead, most of us limp along in pursuit of the momentary success signs of the society we inhabit. You can do better.

Let's go out on a distant limb and suppose that you'd like to be wealthy. Rich and poor are, of course, relative evaluations. Prosperity in one society buys you the best hut, two additional wives, and three additional sheep, while in another society, you're not affluent unless you can afford a summer home in Newport, a mistress or gigolo, and a Lamborghini to tool around in on Sunday afternoons. According to the World Bank, over a billion and a half people make a dollar a day or less. Many in this group worry each day about not having enough food to feed their children. But those who do have enough food, and in particular, more than their neighbors, don't consider themselves poor. Hunger is an absolute concept, but poverty is comparative, as are fame, status, power, and most other objects of our desire.

When we ask ourselves how we're doing, we naturally

compare ourselves against our friends, former classmates, and new acquaintances. Abundant evidence confirms that we care much more about how we rate with our peers than about the size of our incomes or success in an absolute sense. Sometimes we don't measure up well, and the comparison hurts. But rather than mask the pain with Band-Aid excuses, we should focus on the discomfort, because we can turn this unhappy disparity into an opportunity to learn some interesting things about ourselves.

The blessings of envy

It is more desirable to be the handsomest than the wisest man in his majesty's dominions, for there are more people who have eyes than understanding.

—William Hazlitt

We all know about the bad side of envy. It is, after all, one of the seven deadly sins. Justly so, for envy does de-moral-ize your spirit; it makes you feel base and ungracious, and entices you to commit base, ungracious acts. But some philosophers have argued that envy also has its virtuous side when it serves as an impetus for social equality. Our immediate interest here, however, is not the moral status of envy, good or bad, but the use of this emotion as a tool for self-discovery. And in that regard, envy is a blessing. With the concentration of a laser, envy cuts right through our emotional charades.

The clue is this pain. Among all the deadly sins, only envy hurts. (Aristotle notes that even anger is accompanied by pleasant fantasies of revenge.) And there is no mistaking envy's arrival; the ache can be so intense that, as the Roman poet Horace commented, "Sicilian tyrants could never have contrived a better torture." This discomfort is an opportunity. Physical distress serves as an essential warning system; individuals who suffer from an awful neurological disease that disables normal pain sensations can't live very long because they don't notice that disease has invaded their bodies until it is too late. Similarly, the anguish of envy illuminates the most fragile sectors of our self-image. You wouldn't experience physical pain if your body never deteriorated, and you wouldn't experience envy if you never coveted other people's possessions. Achieving emotional perfection, however, is no more likely than achieving physical perfection. Envy is part of our human condition and thus easily provoked; a friend's new car, beau, stock options, or promotion can be enough to set it off.

The good news, as we've said, is that envy can be an emotional eye-opener, if you care to look. It unearths both what really matters to you and where you think you rank in comparison with others. Here is an example of how envy reveals our true feelings.

Ron sells long-distance telephone systems for Sprint and is fairly successful at it. For some reason, though, it's important to Ron that he's perceived as an intellectual, as "more than just a businessman." He'll make sure to let you know a few minutes into your first conversation with him that his college major was comparative literature, and that although he's too busy to read much these days—these years, as it turns out—he still feels most at home in the world of letters. "I know I'm caught up in all this materialism," he says, "but it makes me uncomfortable. It's not what I'm really about."

Really, Ron? I'm driving with him in the most chic neighborhood of Long Island's East Hampton. The few homes that you can see from the road are magnificent structures surrounded by sprawling, immaculate lawns, and you can't help but wonder about the even grander homes hidden at the ends of the long, curved driveways, behind towering hedges. Ron is slavering like a kid with his first cotton candy at a county fair. He enthusiastically points out the tennis courts, comments on every passing Porsche, regales me with tedious stories about all the people he knows who made a mint in the recent bull stock market—like the salesman in his division, three years behind him and certainly no smarter, who made so much money last year that he hired a chauffeur to drive his wife on her shopping expeditions. Hey, Ron, what happened to the treasures of James Joyce and the life of the mind? Why the palpable envy if you don't really care about all this luxury?

Ron isn't unique. We all imagine ourselves as having interests and desires that conform to our ideal selves, but aren't part of our actual wishes. What gets your envy juices flowing? Your brother-in-law with the financial wherewithal to pick himself up in the cold of winter for a holiday break on a Caribbean isle? Your neighbor, who is lucky to have easygoing children? Women your age with fewer wrinkles? Friends with a better education? Envy forces us to own up to our embarrassing cache of desires.

Envy not only makes explicit what implicitly matters to you, but also reveals your expectations, where you think you belong on the scale of ranking. This self-appraisal is how we distinguish envy from fantasy.

Elvira is deep into another daydream. This time her bank statement has just arrived and—look at this—her net worth has increased yet again by millions. She's pleased, and muses to herself, "As I told Bill Gates the other day, few us know firsthand the pleasures of the multibillionaire." But unlike the Microsoft mogul, Elvira's generosity is as legendary as her wealth. She's widely applauded for the gifts she graciously bestows on friends, family, and the needy. Elvira likes that image: good and rich, but also rich and good. In another sweet reverie, Elvira sees herself at the piano, effortlessly gliding her way from Chopin to Ellington. The women in the room can't help noticing how she dazzles the men with her blazing talent compounded with her extraordinary beauty. "She has the ravishing looks of the young Cindy Crawford, but only more so," she overhears one fellow say about her. And they don't even know that she's just completed a new novel, a sure masterpiece.

You hate to wake the girl. Reality is so much less pleasant. Elvira barely manages to pay the rent, and the only thing she shares with Bill Gates is her looks. In the artistic department, she can't carry a tune and hasn't written anything creative since those two poems she composed on her fourteenth birthday. Elvira is not having an encounter with envy but a spin in the make-believe ballroom. We feel the pangs of envy only when we measure ourselves against those we consider our equals or near equals, and notice their successes and our failures. Elvira, and the rest of us mortals, doesn't feel diminished by Gates's extraordinary fortune or Crawford's exceptional beauty. On the other hand, we might very well be envious of our next-door neighbor's income, our sister's talents, and the coworker who has become the new darling of the boss.

As we've suggested, an honest investigation of your envies will reveal what truly matters to you. The more honest your probe, the bigger the payoff in self-under-standing. But once you've completed your introspective sleuthing, it's time to get beyond this reaction. Unchecked envy sours your judgment and gnaws at your joys. Those caught in the grip of what Shakespeare in *Othello* called the "green-eyed monster" are unable to develop healthy ambition. They can never enjoy success, for as Dr. Willard Gaylin explains in his book *Feelings: Our Vital Signs*, "No matter how much good comes to the chronically envious, they still find ways to see themselves as lacking and still look to others who have more."

There will always be others with more of what you want. Live with it. Think, instead, about modifying your aspirations. In all probability, you won't own a mansion or sail the seas in your private yacht, and you definitely will get older and look it; have fights with your parents, spouse, and children; and never get around to doing so much of what you'd love to do. That's called living a real life.

How can you stop contrasting your achievements with those of others? First, we need to take a closer look into the dynamics of envy.

Philosophers distinguish between malicious envy and nonmalicious envy. In nonmalicious envy, I want what you have. I don't begrudge your expansive and expensive apartment, but I sure wish I had one like it. In its healthiest forms, nonmalicious envy becomes admiration and serves as a positive motivator. We want to be as well-read as our friend, have her courage to ask the boss for a raise, or have the confidence of others to quit a job we detest.

When we speak of envy, however, it's usually the malicious kind we have in mind. Here, the attitude isn't merely that I want what you have; I also can't stand the fact that you have it: "I seethe just thinking of that bitch in that BMW with her new Ivy League boyfriend at her side and that stupid grin on her face." The Latin origin of the word "envy," *invidere,* meaning "to look askance at" or "look with spite," captures the flavor of this malice.

Malicious envy can drive ambition—straight into a wall. It begins with distorting our judgments of the people we envy. We can't stand the fact that someone is superior to us with regard to some feature, and desperately seek to reestablish our equality. To our sorrow, we can't attain parity by promoting ourselves. The hard truth is that we aren't as good-looking as our rival, or as rich or as talented. Nor can we easily remove those qualities from our antagonist. As much as we'd like to, we aren't going to scar her face, steal her diamonds, or break the hand she uses to paint those wonderful pictures. Instead, we do what we can—we belittle her achievements so that they appear no better than our own. We say to ourselves, and to anyone who will listen, that her success is undeserved: "Alison's promotion, you know, had nothing to do with merit and everything to do with sucking up." We mock the person's talents: "It's all surface with Cynthia. She's really not that smart. She only learned how to sound intelligent at those fancy schools she attended." We explain away accomplishments as the result of external advantages: "How do you think Stuart got that client? It's all connections." And, in a pinch, we can always attribute our rival's progress to sheer luck.

Envy-driven ambition, therefore, is dishonest at the root. The deceit begins with the judgment of others, then seeps into your own self-estimate; soon you wonder whether you, too, deserve credit for your successes. Uneasy lies the crown of ambition on the envious.

But beware. Envy can be a thorn in your career not only when you are its perpetrator but also when you are its target. When you pursue your own definition of making it, you win the respect of some and the resentment of many. Envy of the rich and famous is obvious and widespread, but few attract as much bitter envy as those who seek their own dreams.

We have little control over family connections, genetic endowment, and the random circumstances that help determine who advances in this life and who does not. But self-determination matters at least as much as these other factors, and that quality is within our dominion.

Therefore, explains psychologist Adrian van Kaam in *Envy and Originality*, people feel threatened by self-motivated individuals. "The original person reminds people of a life that might have been theirs had they not crippled their potential for creative living. Facing the self-motivated man, the impersonal one feels exposed. He feels called upon to be himself. His anonymity is threatened. For an anxious moment, he feels isolated from the daily source of his thought and movement: the anonymous public." When we meet self-possessed people, the contrast with our own lack of independence is unnerving, and so we join the social chorus that calls these individuals eccentric outsiders.

When you go your own way, expect to be on the receiving end of envy's slings and arrows. These barbs will annoy, and they can sting and slow you down, but they won't stop you. Once you divorce your idea of making it from the ambition of others, their hostility loses its bite. For unlike those who envy you, you're comfortable playing the hand you've been dealt, and neither want nor expect to use another's cards. Their insecurity is their problem. Yours is the much more absorbing problem of how to crystallize your objectives and then figure out how to obtain them.

In "A Poet's Advice to Students," e. e. cummings described this challenge as the most difficult of all: "To be nobody but yourself—in a world which is doing its best, night and day, to make you like everybody else—means to fight the hardest battle which any human being can fight, and never stop fighting."

The destructive cunning of competition

Competitions are for horses, not artists.
>—Béla Bartók

I don't meet competition. I crush it.
>—Charles Revson

"What a loser," Jake comments about one person. About another, he says, "He's a bastard, but you've got to admit the bastard's on top."

The competitively ambitious see life as a battlefield from which only two kinds of people emerge: winners and losers. To "make it" is to be among the victors. The central tenet of this persuasion is the doctrine of football's Vince Lombardi: "Winning isn't everything, it's the only thing." A more caustic version of this sentiment is from baseball's Leo Durocher: "Show me a good loser and I'll show you a loser."

For those who see the world this way, competition is the chief motivation in all spheres of their lives, from career moves and business decisions to choice of romantic interest. Life is a network of contests that take the form of what decision theorists call "zero-sum games"; as in poker, what one person loses, the others win. But life's contests, we're reminded, are even starker. Unlike card games, our battles generate few winners but many losers. Only one contestant wins the gold medal, only one candidate is elected to the vacant seat, only one executive is appointed CEO, only a small percentage of applicants are admitted to elite schools, only a tiny fraction are among the superrich. Making it is not easy.

The competitive presumption is smuggled into the workplace under the cloak of metaphor. We habitually describe our career as a "race" to the top that requires clever moves in the "game" of office politics.

"You bet ambition in the workplace is combat," Yolanda says, explaining how she approaches her own career goals. "Competition is what drives corporations in the marketplace and what drives the rat race within a corporation. The way I see it, either I play the game to win or I don't play at all." I ask Yolanda, an accounts manager at a branch of Chase Manhattan, what counts as winning in her case. "No, I don't expect to become the CEO of Chase, and I'm not even sure I'd want to. My aims are high but reasonable, though no doubt they'll change, depending on how things shake out. But I can tell you that they definitely include getting ahead of the rest of the pack I'm with now. I'm sure most of them feel the same way. We're friends and colleagues, but we're rivals, too." It's a hard outlook, but Yolanda insists that those who disagree are confusing sentimentality with reality. "Those misty-eyed idealists who celebrate cooperation together with their entourage of wimps and sore losers aren't singing about the world we inhabit." She thinks tennis star Martina Navratilova had it exactly right when she remarked, "Those who say 'It's not whether you win or lose that counts' probably lost."

These folk are not anomalies. We live in a culture that celebrates competition. Remember the motto plastered on the backs of BMWs in the 1980s and in the hearts of that generation's Yuppies—"Whoever dies with the most toys wins"? The sentiment may have been coarse and perhaps self-mocking, but it did reflect our culture's ethos of acquisition. The decade that followed was hardly less committed to competition. A parade of business books flaunted macho titles about the shark-infested marketplace as they urged us to learn the competitor's golden rule: "Do unto others before they do unto you."

People who devote their energies to getting ahead of others usually justify their behavior by appealing to two popular but untenable myths. One is that competition is a natural condition, and the other is that competition always leads to better outcomes. These unwarranted assumptions need to be dispelled if we are to honestly evaluate the proper role of competition in careers.

Competitiveness is not a mandate of nature

You're watching a nature show on television. On a snowy bank in Scandinavia, two reindeer lock horns in a ferocious contest for dominance, while in a lush savanna ten thousand miles away, a gorilla flashes his teeth in an indubitable display of intimidation. Depictions of mammalian males contending for supremacy are a mainstay of these documentaries and the predominant audience for these programs is men. *Homo sapiens*, goes the claim, is just like other species in this regard; competition is natural for us, too—men and women. The human race is a story about the race between humans.

You can find this argument articulated in the sophisticated jargon of academic journals as well as in its unadorned versions in the neighborhood bar. The verdict is the same: It's as much a competitive jungle here in our well-appointed offices as out there in the wild. Competition is the way of the world.

The evidence, however, suggests otherwise. Sure, you can tie your ambition to getting ahead of others, but this is your choice, not nature's. The evolutionary benefits of cooperative group behavior and altruism are critical to the survival of the individual and his genes. Competition is not the entire story of our species nor of other species. For example, when bonobos, a category of monkeys closely related to humans, get into an altercation, they resolve their differences through sexual intimacy: by making love, not war.

Competition is even less of a biological directive for human beings, for if anthropology defines humans at all, it defines us as social animals. So many of the great accomplishments and disasters in human history are the results of cooperation. Only by working in concert could humans have explored every nook of this planet and peeked at the planets beyond. And, for that matter, no individual acting alone could wreak such havoc on our environment or carry out the brutalities of military campaigns as do men and women acting together. So, too, our daily social life is replete with group acts of kindness as well as criminality; one minute we help an old person cross the street, and the next minute we're rude without cause to someone else. Hormones are not the overriding influence in competitive aggression, as many suppose. Indeed, among animals, testosterone, the hormone associated with aggressiveness, increases at the end of a fight, not at its beginning. So, too, with people. In his provocative survey of the human condition, anthropologist Marvin Harris points to a variety of studies that found a decrease of testosterone among college wrestlers *before* their matches, but an increase in testosterone in young men just *after* they received their medical degrees. Harris also reminds us of eunuchs who had illustrious careers as commanders of armies and were widely feared for their ferocity in battle.

To be sure, competitiveness is a fact of life in our culture. It defines our education, our games, and our business. No doubt, we operate in a marketplace where jockeying for position is often a ruthless undertaking. But even here, competitiveness is only one aspect of the market among many. Neither nature nor culture compels us to make competition the dominant drive in our ambitions.

Competition does not improve performance

The assumption that competition fosters maximum performance is even more popular than the appeal to nature. It is equally spurious.

The studies are comprehensive, canvassing the spectrum of professions and skills. They cut across age and gender, and their results have been steadily replicated. The conclusion is surprising: Individuals who are motivated by competitiveness do less well than those who have other motivations, such as self-mastery.

Competition diminishes creativity. In one representative

study, girls aged seven to eleven were asked to make collages. One group competed and the other group did not. A panel of professional artists rated the results and found that the work of the children who competed was less spontaneous, less complex, and "significantly less creative than those made by children in the control group."

Competition also seems to undermine the quality of one's work. Robert Helmreich of the University of Texas examined the publishing records of more than one hundred individuals with Ph.D.s in science. Those who rated high on the measurement of interest in their work and self-imposed goals did significantly more quality work than those who ranked high on the competitive scale. Helmreich observed the same pattern when he investigated the performance of airline pilots, reservation agents, and seven other types of jobholders. Even more astonishing are studies discussed by Jeffery J. Martin and Diane L. Gill in *Journal of Sport and Exercise Psychology*, which suggest that even in sports, the bastion of competition, the incentive to win is not the optimum motivation. Athletes who focus on personal performance goals—to shoot 70 percent from the free-throw line, say, or run a mile fifteen seconds faster than the previous month—shoot better and run faster than athletes who concentrate on beating their opponents.

This pattern holds true in the business world as well. Janet Spence, a former president of the American Psychological Association, undertook a study comparing business executives who scored as relatively noncompetitive with strongly competitive executives. Her results were intriguing: The noncompetitive group of executives earned, on average, 16 percent more than the competitive group. While competition might increase efficiency across organizations, what works well on the corporate "macro" level doesn't necessarily work as well for individuals.

Upon reflection, these findings are not so surprising. When winning is everything, or even the primary thing, you are disinclined to take risks that might jeopardize your front-runner status. Instead, you coast. But coasting is never the technique of excellence; it is, rather, a prescription for failure. We are all familiar with the sad tale of the once-thriving business that goes belly up because its owners could not accept that what brought them to first place in the old days wouldn't sustain them in the present.

Think about where you want to go in what remains of your career. "Being better than" shouldn't be part of your conclusion. If you allow yourself to thrive only when you are in the thick of a heated competition, you will not thrive often; few careers (thankfully) sustain that intense rivalry. We do better when self-mastery, not winning, is the objective. And in the global work market, self-mastery will guide your career even when heated competition isn't there to spur you on.

How do we develop ambitions that track accomplishments of our own choosing and are suitable to our personal values? How do we overcome the insidious competitiveness that is so much a part of our world? How can you make competition work for you, not against you? Here are a few suggestions.

Don't compete with competitive people

Do you sometimes find yourself in the midst of an argument with people whom you have no interest in debating? You feel trapped. And you are. Arguers maneuver you into defending your refusal to get into a dispute, and before you realize how you got snookered, you're raising your voice in a heated exchange. Similarly, social psychologists note that competitive people are more likely to get noncompetitive people to compete with them than cooperative people are to get competitive people to cooperate. As you no doubt can attest, in the world of work, collaborations regularly turn into competitions, and the process by which this happens is often subtle. You need to keep your radar constantly on to detect when you're being sucked into unwanted competition.

Remember that careers are not zero-sum games

The Olympic runner in the hundred-meter dash crosses the finish line a nanosecond behind the winner of the race and is declared the loser. He is the second fastest person on the planet, but is deemed a loser!

We live in a social environment where most institutions are structured as pyramids. In corporations, for example, the person perched on top is the big winner, and everyone else, from the next in line down to the multitudes on the bottom, are all, in varying degrees, losers. You don't have to measure success this way.

Lives and careers have room for many winners. There's a place for everyone in heaven (and hell, too), and admission doesn't prevent others from entering; indeed, your assistance to others helps determine your own eligibility. Ambition is not a zero-sum game either—reaching your destination doesn't preclude others from reaching theirs. It is foolhardy to pose a competitive goal for yourself that allows for only one winner, so why stack the deck against yourself? It makes more sense, surely, to formulate more generous goals that invite others to succeed along with you.

Inclusive ambitions are also more honest. We protect ourselves against unfavorable social comparisons by constructing fables. Studies reveal that when people lose a contest, they tend to exaggerate the ability of those who outperformed them. By aggrandizing their rivals, they maintain their self-esteem in the face of defeat: "Hey, I lost, but she was in another league." Winners, too, inflate the ability of their opponents to make themselves look even better. Other research demonstrates that competitive people more often excuse themselves for their failures and blame bad luck for their defeat.

Compete cooperatively

The word *competition* comes from the Latin *competere*, which means "to strive together." Sparring partners, jogging partners, learning partners all compete in this original sense of pacing one another. This is competition that brings out the best in both persons.

You can see a wonderful illustration of this in pickup games of basketball. A group of guys are shooting around. After a few minutes of this casual play, someone suggests that they play a game. Teams are devised with an eye on creating "even sides." Evenly matched teams are more fun than lopsided talent, for unlike professional sports, the point of the game here is not to win, but to play. The participants often forget to keep track of the score, and there is little incentive to cheat. And in contradistinction to pro ball, members of team A will congratulate a player on team B for his exceptional play and rush to his aid if he is hurt. Pickup matches are certainly competitive, but the rewards are in the activity itself, not external rewards as in the form of pay. This is the kind of competition that doesn't alienate you from what you are doing. It would be wonderful to bring this spirit of cooperative competitiveness into our work life.

We often do our best in our leisure and our work when we have partners who spur us on. We come up with niftier words in a game of Boggle or improve our backhand slice in tennis. At work, a supportive competition can challenge us to come up with creative solutions and to go the extra mile on the assignment. But this requires an association in which the participants truly root for each other and celebrate each other's progress. This isn't commonplace—if you do enjoy a mutually supportive relationship of this kind with someone at work, you've got something worth cherishing and cultivating.

A final word on competition and envy. Both competitiveness and envy chain you to other people. Focusing on the success of those around you diverts you from your own advancement. But let's not be glib about this. Breaking free from these comparisons is incredibly difficult. Much of the time, you may feel left behind. Much of the time you will feel lost, moving without a clear direction. It's not easy to persevere when no one else shares your path.

However, the only way to really succeed is to have a self-formed and self-sustained ambition. And that comes from having a clear understanding of what you really want from your work and career. So what *do* you want? Status? Power? For many, the first and final motivation to work is money.

THE SEDUCTIONS OF SUCCESS: MONEY, POWER, AND LEADERSHIP

Let me introduce myself. I am a man who at the precocious age of thirty-five experienced an astonishing revelation: it is better to be a success than a failure. Money, I now saw (no one, of course, has ever seen it before), was important: it was better to be rich than to be poor. Power, I now saw (moving on to higher subtleties), was desirable: it was better to give orders than to take them. Fame, I now saw (how courageous of me not to flinch), was unqualifiedly delicious: it was better to be recognized than anonymous.

—Norman Podhoretz, *Making It*

What is my loftiest ambition? I've always wanted to throw an egg at an electric fan.

—Anon.

Making Money (in) Your Life

Money is the root of all evil, and everyone needs roots.

Old rich guy to his young mistress: "Would you love me even if I wasn't so generous?"
Young mistress: "Yes, I'd love you. And miss you dearly."

There's not much to say about money that hasn't been said. You've probably heard it all: the quips, the slogans, the jokes, the grandmotherly advice, and the profound insights. We talk incessantly about money and especially how we need more of it.

I don't trust people when they discuss their feelings about money. I don't trust myself either. It's too easy to lie when it comes to this subject. The truth is that I'm not sure how much being rich matters to me. Although I've never been good at making the big bucks, the idea of being wealthy sure does sound appealing. But my friends tell me that this clearly isn't something I want all that badly. "Your attraction is too abstract," they say. "If money was important to you, you'd work a lot harder at getting it. But you don't. You write philosophical books instead."

Well, I'm not so sure. I oscillate between thinking that my daydreams of a life free of financial worries are just fanciful wishes I share with nearly everyone on the planet, and thinking that this is a worthwhile, achievable aspiration that I ought to pursue. Some days I worry about "selling out"; other days I call it "buying in." My attitude toward making money seems to fluctuate with the color of the room's drapes. I suspect this vacillation is true of most people, and perhaps of you, too.

How much does money matter? On your pro-capital days, you're the "realist" who recognizes that money, not love, makes the world go round; in any case, money can buy love a whole lot faster than love can buy money. You notice that "money talks, everything else mumbles," and when it's money talking, everyone pays close attention. You point out that even if money can't always buy what you need, it can, at least, buy what you want, and that's a lot more than can be said for poverty. Feeling crummy? A few hours on the Concorde for dinner in Paris does wonders for your mood. Solid assets, you realize, buy life's dearest delights, including intangibles like esteem. As the ancient proverb has it, "When you're rich, not only are you handsome, but you sing well, too."

If this sounds too crude, you can fly the lofty route without leaving the pro-green camp. You're not defending greed. Affluence and integrity, you insist, are not mutually exclusive. Our religious heritage expressly deems riches, honestly gained, a sign of God's grace. Why can't business be a noble calling? What's wrong with making money? Weren't the patriarchs Abraham, Isaac, and Jacob blessed with livestock and cattle, and none the less holy for their prosperity?

But in other moods, the primacy of money disturbs you. You find the respect paid to the dollar by nearly all segments of society downright contemptible—sure, money talks, but it would be nice if sometimes it listened.

Your reservations about the quest for the gold may also trace to religious sources. The New Testament does, after all, declare the love of money to be the root of all evil, a notion you find increasingly persuasive as you survey the modern consumer culture that surrounds you. Who can deny that our ceaseless grasping for wealth exercises a pernicious power over our lives? It defaces our dignity, turns up our ugliest side—for the sake of the dollar, people steal, extort, torture, kidnap, and murder. (Manifesting the connection we draw between avarice and evildoing, notice how we generally consider it worse to commit crimes out of greed than out of hatred, say, or ideological commitment.) When you're in one of these anti-materialist turns, you resolve to break free from the ever-tempting cultural addiction to owning more and consuming more.

So which of these two attitudes is the reasonable one? They both are. Both responses to money strike sympathetic chords in our ambitions. We can and do live with the incompatibility.

The embrace of a positive and a negative attitude toward money is less wishy-washy than it seems. True, for some people, the dollar is always a top priority, while it never is for others—monks aren't the only ones uninterested in becoming rich. For most of us, though, the tug of money waxes and wanes over the years, sometimes taking center stage, sometimes receding to the background. Most of the time, though, we judge wealth as but one luxury among others; a good thing, but not everything. Our own mixed feelings should make us wary of rendering sweeping moral judgments about the importance of money in other people's lives.

Consider the tale of Carla and Marla. Both women are now in their sixties. Neither ever married. Carla was always profligate, spending her salary as soon as it arrived. Fine wine flowed at her lavish parties. The elegant decor of her apartment always spelled "expensive"; fresh, exotic flowers were a regular touch. Carla enjoyed the theater and good restaurants, and never skimped on her many travels to the far corners of the planet. But now, Carla's income has dwindled to meager stipends, and her former grand lifestyle has, perforce, been reduced to a level just above the edge of poverty. Marla, in contrast, rarely spent money on herself. Her clothing and furniture were always modest. She never took trips on her vacations—and you could count on one hand the number of times she went out for an evening's entertainment. Instead, Marla saved her earnings and invested wisely. As a result, she can live the rest of her life in secure comfort.

Neither of these women envies the other. Each thinks the other lived foolishly. But interpersonal judgments are inappropriate here; not everyone has to live the same life. Some folks care most about comfort, others prefer free time, and still others dedicate themselves to amassing a fortune. What matters is not so much whether you choose to make wealth a centerpiece of your career but whether this choice reflects your own values and not those of people around you.

Is becoming rich part of "making it" for you? More pointedly: Would you consider your career or life a failure if you didn't become affluent?

One way to measure your affection for money is to play the trade-off game, a favorite among psychologists and domineering party hostesses. You're offered a series of hypothetical swaps of cash for other qualities. For example, for ten million dollars, would you:

Accept a permanent ugly scar on your face?

Leave your country and never return?

Leave your spouse and family?

Go to jail for ten years?

Give up fifteen points of your IQ?

Bark on a busy street every morning for five minutes, for five years?

Break someone's arms and legs?

Perhaps you'd cut the deal for some of these offers, perhaps for none, perhaps you'd answer differently at different times in your life. While these exchanges are hypothetical and may be unrealistic, they illuminate an essential characteristic of careers: We constantly face trade-offs. The choice is rarely ten million dollars to deface our bodies, but many of us do have to choose between, say, increased income and job opportunity versus moving away from friends and families. To make these decisions intelligently, you need to be clear about what provides you with your deepest satisfactions. Monetary maturity is not about learning how much of your money to invest to make money, but about how much of your life to invest to make money. In other words, money matters . . . but not that much.

Two kinds of people, and two kinds only, affect to despise money: those who have more than they need and those who secretly believe, if they have not already had it proven to them, that they are unable to obtain enough of it. Much the greater part of mankind, whose reactions to money range from open obsession with it to a pretense of disinterest live in various stages of thrall to this extraordinary invention.

—Jason Epstein

Money isn't everything, but it ranks up there with oxygen.

—Rita Davenport

We may love money, but why do we call the wealthy "filthy rich?" Freud believed that the association of money with dirt lies deep in our psyche and our neurotic compulsions, as he suggests in his influential analysis "Little Hans and the Rat Man." He notes that in ancient civilizations, in myths, fairy tales, and superstitions, in unconscious thinking, in dreams and neurosis, money is brought into an intimate relationship with dirt. More precisely, with dung. Look closely, for example, at those Brueghel paintings of peasant life, and you'll notice that gold is depicted as human turd.

This extreme degradation of money is surely a reaction to the extreme adulation on the other pole, and it's just as puerile. A few individuals might reach such heights of soulfulness that material opulence has no allure for them, but when the rest of us express wholesale disdain for wealth, you can assume that less noble motives are in operation. More likely, such sentiments express frustration or a refusal to grow up and accept responsibility. Let's face it: Poverty isn't romantic. Aristotle, his common sense evident as usual, notes in his *Nichomechean Ethics* how difficult it is to be happy when you must expend so much effort just to secure enough food and shelter to survive. We don't have to starve, however, to know how anxieties about money exhaust our energies and good humor.

So it comes down to a question of degree. Just how important is being rich to you, and how rich do you need to be?

Your monetary worth

The notion that money can't buy happiness is a fallacy. As a matter of fact happiness is the only thing it can buy. It can't buy you style, intelligence, or beauty or wit or affection or respect, but it can definitely buy you happiness. And the happiness it can't buy it can rent.

—Quentin Crisp

There are no universal truths about money to help us devise our own priorities. Other cultures place higher status on other values, such as salvation, power, beauty, adventure, or inventiveness. While it's easy to notice how much our Western culture places a premium on wealth, we often don't recognize just how arbitrary we are in deeming which qualities are financially rewarded and which are not.

Consider excellences of the body. At present, the ability to throw a baseball sixty feet, six inches, at a speed of ninety-seven miles per hour or more will bring you an income of several million dollars a year. On the other hand, skill at throwing a discus, a talent that garnered glory in ancient Greece, will now fetch only minor, fleeting notice at the Olympic Games and no financial gains whatsoever.

Difficulty of the task is not the issue. The champion handball player isn't less athletic than the champion golfer. Rewards are determined, rather, by the fickle interests of the marketplace. The fact that you can spit wooden nickels across the gym floor, or stand on your head for ten hours while singing the entire repertoire of the Beatles, or hold your breath for a minute and a half, or lift a Toyota Camry will astonish your friends and might get you into *The Guinness Book of Records*. Perhaps it will be otherwise in some other time and some other place, but here and now these accomplishments bring you neither fame nor fortune.

The criteria for turning psychological abilities into hard currency are as arbitrary as those regarding physical skills. No doubt, you realized long ago that people who are successful at making money aren't smarter than the rest of us but only smarter at making money. (And even that isn't always so—never underestimate the luck factor.) Cleverness, of course, helps in business; for example, ability with numbers is a plus, as is a facility for persuasion. But brilliance has little to do with financial success, as so many acclaimed middle-class theoretical physicists and even poorer poets can attest.

This observation might seem utterly pedestrian, a restatement of the obvious. But it's easy to forget that we don't always get paid for having the qualities we most cherish. For example, suppose you're an exceptional lover. This aptitude enriches your life along with the lives of those fortunate individuals with whom you share your talent. But unless you have a certain night job, your skill will do little to help increase your investment portfolio.

So, too, you might value your compassion, but empathy isn't a bankable endowment, and you wouldn't want to exploit it this way. Similarly, you won't get a raise for being an outstanding parent or an abiding friend. In fact, few of the character traits and abilities that make you proud of yourself translate directly into hard cash.

Our decisions about how much money we need and what we are prepared to give up to get it will change as we face new options. Here, however, are three aspects of money that you should bear in mind whenever you evaluate the worth of money in your career and life:

- Wealth is an inherently elastic concept.

- Satisfying your wealth quotient depends on how much money you had before.

▪ The worth of your money is invariably measured against that of your peers.

Let's consider each of these features of money.

My moneyed friend Bensy calls it "the number." This, he explains to me, is the number of millions of dollars one must have to be considered wealthy by the wealthy. He assures me that when he obtains "the number," he will retire from his frenetic business life and return to his abandoned talent with the clarinet. Bensy has been telling me this for decades. He means it, but like the distant horizon, "the number" keeps receding as he gets closer. I remember when it was three million; then, when he reached that goal, it suddenly became five; then ten; and now, I believe "the number" is in the vicinity of twenty million dollars. Infinity, here we come.

You don't have to be rich to get trapped by the endless elasticity of money. Economist H. F. Clark found that no matter what their level of income, Americans want, on average, to make 25 percent more and, as you'd guess, when they get there, they're ready, of course, for the next 25 percent increase. "Riches enlarge appetites," Clark concludes, "they don't shrink it."

The second characteristic of wealth to keep in mind as you formulate your ambitions is that the worth of a dollar to you today depends on how much money you had previously. Adaptation theory postulates that we judge our current prosperity relative to what we have become accustomed to. At some level, incremental increases cease to be very satisfying; going from rich to very rich isn't as exciting as going from average to rich.

This relativity applies to consumer satisfaction as well, and explains why we are easily jaded. In the past couple of decades, the United States has seen an increase of 484 percent in the number of air conditioners in the country, a 134 percent increase in freezers, 356 percent in clothes dryers, and 743 percent in dishwashers. But who now gets a buzz from owning these appliances, or a television or a computer? We're already looking to the next gadget—we already *need* the next gadget—whatever that may be. In his classic book *The Theory of the Leisure Class*, written in 1899, Thorstein Veblen observed that our attitude toward consumer goods is intimately tied to our social status: "In modern society, members of each stratum accept as their ideal of decency the scheme of life in vogue in the next higher stratum. So what people once thought of as luxuries they now think of as necessities." Indeed—the consumer treadmill is predicated by there being no permanently satisfied customers.

Finally, keep in mind as you calculate the value of money that we judge the worth of our wealth not by what we own, but in comparison with what our peers own. In his influential book *The Social Limits to Growth*, Fred Hirsch argued that once survival needs are accounted for, it is "positional goods" that matter to us. The differential in value between an old Chevy and a new Jaguar is not the horsepower—both cars get you to the mall—but the status each confers. What we mean by saying our child goes to a "good" school is that she goes to a school which performs well as measured by the schools our friends' children attend. The next question, then, is Whom do you see as your peers? Do you want to be the proverbial big fish in a small pond or the small fish in a big pond? No matter how we answer, we will appraise our worth by comparing our assets against those we consider to be in our league.

We can draw a few summary conclusions about money and ambition. Money does make life easier. So do good looks. And a great education. And outstanding health. And loving parents. And good friendships. And ten thousand other features of a wholesome life. We also noted that while we absolutely need money, money's worth is not absolute. Its value depends on what we had before, and with whom we compare ourselves. We need to recognize, too, that the law of diminishing returns operates here—the more money we have, the less it satisfies. Maturity comes—and for some it never does—when you accept that no one can have it all. Some will choose to exchange much of life's bounty for financial riches, but others take to heart Ralph Waldo Emerson's warning that "money often costs too much."

The presumptions of power

So long as a man's power is bound to the goal, the work, the calling, it is, in itself, neither good nor evil, only a suitable or unsuitable instrument. But as soon as this bond with the goal is broken or loosened, and the man ceases to think of power as the capacity to do something, but thinks of it as a possession, then his power, being cut-off and self-satisfied, is evil and corrupts the history of the world.

—Martin Buber

Perched on the loftiest throne in the world, we are still sitting on our own behind.

—Michel de Montaigne

Tycoons are driven to their wealth by various motives. Many seek it for the luxuries it buys, but others are especially drawn to the power that comes with money. For them, control, not gold, is the object of desire. But money is just one of many routes to power—other paths, such as titles, fame, position, and marriage have their own allure.

Is the "will to power" part of your ambitions? The longing for power is even more embarrassing than the craving for affluence, and we are especially self-deceptive about our feelings on this subject. As we shape our ambitions and their connection to our lives, we need to ratchet up our self-honesty and reflect on what attracts us to power and what repels us.

For example, would you like to own a slave? Suppose, as was true for most of human history, slavery was legal and socially acceptable. It's hard to imagine what it feels like to have total dominion over another person, to own someone else's time and body, but does the idea, however dark and uneasy, sound at all attractive?

Passing fantasies of mastery of others are not uncommon. You might wish at times that you had the magical power to make people drop dead merely by pronouncing "Die! Die!" under your breath. (This wish has a definite urgency when we're behind the steering wheel.) But most of us can see why these stirrings are best kept locked in one's imagination. We know too well of the would-be dictators who strut the world's streets barking orders in their impotent daydreams, and of those among them who manage to cross the border from reverie to actual power, leaving misery and death in their wake.

The prospect of total control over another person may make you uncomfortable, even repulse you, but nonetheless, you may be eager for limited, legitimate power: You don't want to own a plantation with lots of slaves, but you're ready to become the company's CEO. The enticement goes beyond the prestige and stellar income. You like the prerogative of making policy; of deciding whom to promote and demote, hire and fire; of determining what others do and don't do. Being in command not only can requisition so many gifts for its holder—as Henry Kissinger famously observed, "There is no aphrodisiac like power"—but for some, it is a compelling rush in itself. "Better to rule in hell than serve in heaven," wrote John Milton in *Paradise Lost*. Power is powerful.

The drive for power figures very strongly in Charlene's ambitions. She is the manager of a Blockbuster store, but tells me that she has definite plans to move up in the video chain's hierarchy. "Control is, without question, definitely part of what I want. I know that some people think of this as a male thing. Baloney! I think everybody who wants to get ahead is driven to a large extent by a desire for power. I don't need to be queen of the realm. What I want is screw-you power. That's like screw-you money—if you've just won the lottery, you can go to the boss you detest and finally tell her what a jerk she is. You no longer need the job, so you don't care if she fires you. When you have enough power to help or hurt people in your company, they're less likely to mess with you. That's what I mean by screw-you power." Charlene wants me to understand that it isn't just security she's after. "The real charge," she says, "comes from being in charge. From making decisions, not having them made for you. I can do some of that now. I'm fair, but the people under me know that I can make their lives miserable if they don't do their jobs. I'd be lying if I said I don't enjoy instilling this fear."

A desire for power for its own sake does not make for a healthy ambition. This is true no matter what guise the power adopts.

We can distinguish between power as brute force and power as authority. Political theorists call the first kind of clout de facto, power in fact. Remember the old joke that asks, What do you call a six-foot-five, mean-looking bastard who pulls you into an alleyway and puts a knife to your throat? You call him "Sir." This is the de facto tyranny of Saddam Hussein, mobsters, abusive husbands, and garden-variety bullies.

The other type of power is de jure, by law. This is the appeal of authority, power backed by legitimacy. Any stranger can scream at an annoying child zooming around the supermarket aisles, but only the parent has the authority to physically restrain him. Both the gangster and the police officer carry the persuasive argument of a gun in his hand, but only the cop, with due limitations, has the right to use it. Jobs, too, provide authority. By dint of his or her position, the teacher sends the student out of the classroom for misbehaving, the store manager decides the work schedule for the sales personnel, the taxi dispatcher determines which car makes the next pickup, and the judge sentences the convicted criminal to the electric chair.

When the thrill of power comes from "instilling fear," as Charlene implies, you need to pause before making this part of your career goals. To make a long and complicated psychological story short and succinct: The satisfaction of intimidating another person stems from sadistic streaks and revenge fantasies, not from the features of our character that deserve to be nurtured. It doesn't take much psychological insight to see that a need to dominate is a sign of weakness, not strength.

Whether the urge to control is manifested de facto by a pistol or de jure by a job title, the satisfactions of dominance are recognizably adolescent and inane. The bruising bully in the bar thinks he's tough because he can browbeat the smaller patrons. But the bully in the boardroom with his silk shirts and red suspenders who gets off by giving orders is just the suit version of the saloon brawler. And it doesn't matter if the urge to control is exercised through coercion or through the "soft power" of suggestion and attraction. Abraham Lincoln observed that "Nearly all men can stand adversity, but if you want to test a man's character, give him power." He might have added that a person's character is also tested by his or her *ambition* for power.

Power is one thing, influence is another. As members of

a human community, we constantly help shape the beliefs and habits of the people we live with, just as they contour our own attitudes and opinions. Even if we eschew power, we do want our lives to have meaning to others. Influence, however, is many-hued; sometimes immediate and overt, sometimes subtle and distant. We are, like it or not, for better or worse, role models to our children, and our behavior often defines our friendships. The prophet and the thinker, the visionary artist and the pioneering entrepreneur, on the other hand, alter the lives of people they never know, generations yet unborn. One group of people, however, wants to exert influence intentionally and directly. They aspire to leadership.

The Yoke of Leadership

The very highest leader is barely known by men.
Then comes the leader they know and love.
Then the leader they fear.
Then the leader they despise.

—Lao-tzu

Social scientists have a long list of inflated beliefs we have of ourselves, and in the top group is a belief about our leadership abilities. The overwhelming majority of people are convinced they have what it takes to become a superior leader. No wonder leadership is a boom business. Type in "leadership" on your Internet search engine, and hundreds of "leadership consulting companies" will fill your screen. Courses on leadership are the rage in business schools across the country. Each year, thousands of seminars and training programs, along with hundreds of books on the subject, attract the attention and dollars of managers of all ranks. The content is much the same: a standard speech about how leaders are made, not born, followed by experts presenting their respective versions of "ten steps to great leadership." With slight linguistic variations on the basic theme, we are once again instructed that the old-fashioned top-down models of management are now defunct, and in their place we need a new "leadership style" that "empowers" employees.

The rhetorical shift from manager to project leader, team coordinator, and facilitator reflects a growing awareness of a new reality. Back in the late sixteenth century, Francis Bacon told us "Knowledge is power," and the contemporary marketplace is ratifying that insight. We are in the midst of a dramatic transformation from an economy based on the production of things to one based on the production of data. Manipulators of information comprise the fastest-growing segment among current workers; they are diverse and dispersed, determined and direct, and ungovernable by old-style administrative dictates. As a result, corporate executives can no longer act as if they are the ones bestowing the favors. Since his seminal 1959 book, *Landmarks of Tomorrow*, in which he coined the term "knowledge workers," Peter Drucker has maintained that "organizations need knowledge workers more than knowledge workers need organizations." To keep their employees sharp and satisfied, businesses increasingly reward the self-starters and encourage intrapreneurial programs within their companies. The boss of the past, who commanded, "Go," must become the leader who says, "Let's go." The dynamics of organizational leadership has no choice but to change to keep pace.

We can leave the details on how best to implement these shifts in administration to the workshops and those who run them. Our concern here is not how you can get your staff to produce efficiently, but an understanding of leadership in our personal ambitions (though we sometimes forget that managers, too, have worrisome personal careers).

We need to distinguish between managing and leadership. In ordinary language, managing implies, after all, just getting by. "Thank you, I'm managing all right," we say to our friends who ask about our well-being during a crisis. Managing is surviving, not thriving. But we can aim to do more than merely manage our lives. We have a life to *lead*. So, too, we can hope to have careers that excite and enrich, not merely remain afloat.

Some see their personal fulfillment in leading others. The process is the same: You begin by leading yourself. Leadership is an activity rather than a status. It operates by influence, not power; by suggestion, not intimidation; by modeling, not demanding. "Followship" must be earned; it cannot be commanded.

The folk literatures of many cultures have a story that

makes this point succinctly. This is one version: A young man named Agbar tells his guru that he had a dream in which thousands of people flocked to him and proclaimed him their teacher. The guru tells the ambitious fellow that he'd be more impressed if a thousand people had a dream in which Agbar was their teacher.

Leading your life entails all the risks of the pioneer, and leading it well requires a strong intuition about how to get to where you want to go. We lead others with the same vision. In *Mind-Set Management: The Heart of Leadership*, Samuel A. Culbert writes: "If you want to manage effectively, stop trying to get people to be what you want them to be. Engage them where they actually are." This is good advice for administrators, but not for leaders. Genuine leaders engage people not only by showing them where they are but also by pointing to where they might go and how to get there.

If leading other people is part of your idea of "making it," you need to understand clearly what sustains that goal. In the epigraph at the beginning of this section, the theologian Martin Buber says that influence over others is neutral and derives its value from the worth of its destination; influence for its own sake is always a pernicious motive. In other words, you can't just want to lead; you have to want to lead somewhere.

On the other hand, you may not care to lead. You'd rather not have that additional responsibility. You might prefer popularity, or love, or admiration. Ambitions that include leadership are not better or worse than those that don't. They are just different.

As never before, careers in the twenty-first century will demand personal definitions of success and failure. We will have to learn to accept, deep in our gut, the legitimacy of other people's ambitions. This isn't to be confused with tolerance. We tolerate another when we allow the person to have her say even though we think she is wrong. But it isn't wrong to strive for wealth, or not to strive for wealth. It is neither wrong to want to be a leader, nor a defect in ambition to have no such desire. Some folks care about these things, some don't. True, many ambitions share certain aims, such as a concern with status. In *The Human Career: The Self in the Symbolic World*, Walter Goldschmidt, an anthropologist who has studied a broad array of human groups, suggests that "the idea of prestige, the recognition of individual merit, is the very soul of the social order." But there is no universal content by which societies and individuals size up status; no one shoe fits all. Some would rather be the most esteemed professor at Wyoming State College than "just another" professor at MIT. The larger lesson is that there is no one right way to live a life . . . or carve out a career.

MAKING IT IN THE TWENTY-FIRST CENTURY

Everybody wants to be somebody; nobody wants to grow.
—Johann Goethe

Living without markers

Successful management of our new entrepreneurial careers includes the fundamental challenge of determining what counts as success. As we've seen, the traditional emblems of "making it" no longer apply, and the symbols of accomplishment are increasingly unclear. We realize that financial riches don't automatically translate into a rich life, that power at work doesn't preclude weakness in other parts of one's life, and that you often have to choose between winning respect and winning affection. Many of us already experience this private uncertainty in judging our careers. Some of us are high markers and go easy on ourselves; others are tough, stern graders; and more and more of us oscillate between feeling that we're doing well and feeling that we're severely underachieving.

How are you supposed to know how you're doing? According to whose standards? Don't expect an objective appraisal from your friends, because they're as confused as the rest of us. Laura's puzzlement is typical.

"That's my two daughters, Katy and Nora," Laura says, pointing to a photograph partially covered by sticky notes and surrounded by memos and calendars. Her cubicle is small and crowded. The desk is too compact for both work folders and a picture frame. The lack of space bothers Laura less than the lack of privacy, but neither is what she misses most.

Four years ago Laura was a litigator at one of New York's top law firms, where she made oodles of money working oodles of hours. Associates regularly put in sixty hours a week, and the more macho among them clocked significantly more. Laura decided to snip her golden handcuffs and escape to a less feverish career as a program administrator in a university. The time with her small children was just too precious to squander, and her husband's income allowed them to maintain the basics of their lifestyle. Laura doesn't regret the move, but it hasn't been easy.

"It's not the money, though that sure was nice," Laura explains. "And although I'm working in a university setting, the truth is I used my brain a lot more as a lawyer than I do now, and I'm surprised by how much I actually miss thinking harder. To be honest, the dignity thing does weigh on me, too. It's demeaning to spend my day in this tiny open cubicle, especially when former colleagues and my children come to visit. I'm sure that having had a private office makes the adjustment all the more difficult. But I'll get over it. The really hard part about the change? It's not having tags to help me judge how I'm doing in my career. In law firms, as in most structured jobs, you have a title, a salary, and other clear signposts that reflect your status; you can see who and what's above you, and who and what's below. I miss these milestones.

"So some mornings I wake up and say to myself, 'You know, Laura, this isn't bad: You get to spend time with the children, you have a job that helps people, and most of your coworkers are pleasant company. This is a good thing to be doing at this point in your life.' But other mornings I deliver a very different speech: 'Face it, Laura, you're going nowhere. The time you have with the family is wonderful, though sometimes it's also a pain in the butt.

Career-wise, though, you walked away from the big leagues to become just another elevated functionary in the minors. What happened to the glorious aspirations? Instead, you settled for a routine, mezzanine life.' The weird thing is how both perspectives make sense to me."

Don't mistake Laura's career anxiety for insecurity. Her pendulum swings are reasonable for someone who previously worked in an organization with well-defined tiers and now finds herself without such markers. This is especially true for women who have chosen to take a break from the career treadmill, fully aware of how difficult it will be to climb back on. The legions of self-employed also proceed with constant doubts and few guidelines to chart their progress. This is Dennis's situation.

Dennis, a Chicago-based photographer, describes his work as eclectic. "I shoot photographs of clothes for catalogs. That's the bread-and-butter gig that pays for the rent, child support, and upgrade of equipment. But the artistic satisfaction and, I hope, the future big-time money come from my portraits of up-and-coming rock bands."

Dennis is especially proud of his two recent CD covers and a photo spread in a national rap magazine, but he is less sanguine about the direction of his career. "Sometimes I see myself as a competent, steady professional, a late starter with promise. Other times, though, I think I'm just another drudge photographer with the usual fantasies of fame and fortune that are more unlikely with each passing year."

As careers become more fluid and the zigzags in our lives more pronounced, more of us will share Laura's and Dennis's uncertainty about our progress. We will need to chart our way without being able to rely on clearly posted signs that tell us how far we've advanced toward our goals. We can expect our careers to toss about in a world full of plausible options and constant trade-offs. Some floundering will be a natural phase. But at some point, each of us will have to get clear about where we want to go with our careers, what we consider to be our personal achievement, and how we want to go about getting to these goals.

The criteria for making it will be your own, as they will be for each individual. But whatever your definition of success and failure, it should emphasize two critical aspects of the entrepreneurial career:

- You are not responsible for attaining your aims but only for doing your best to achieve them.

- Your idea of the successful career reflects your own values, so the integrity of your character must always be paramount.

Success is in the effort

It is good to have an end to journey toward; but it is the journey that matters in the end.

—Ursula Le Guin

When we envisage ourselves as having made it, we picture ourselves sitting behind our desks, our money piled in the bank, and our family life full of smiles and content-ment. We are respected, honored, maybe even envied.

But whatever the content (and, as we've emphasized, the specifics of success will differ from person to person), this daydream bypasses the most important features of a thriving career. It neglects the adventure, the choices we make and risks we take along the way. It neglects the joy of the trip. After all, no one can guarantee you happiness, but you *can* guarantee your pursuit of happiness. So, too, success is never assured, but you can make sure that you've made the attempt.

Most of us are familiar with Paul Gauguin's paintings and his importance in the history of modern painting, but few are aware that "the case of Gauguin" has become a reference point in recent debates in moral theory. Gauguin had both a family to support and a consuming desire to paint. The two demands were in conflict: Gauguin could earn only a pittance from his art, hardly enough to feed his wife and children. Painting won the conflict. Gauguin left Paris for the enchanted isles of Tahiti, where he produced magnificent, color-rich images of native life. The disagree-ment among moral philosophers is whether the pursuit of art can be justified when it entails abandoning one's fam-ily, or as the question is more abstractly framed: Do moral obligations always outweigh other obligations?

We need to emphasize that Gauguin's contribution to art cannot figure in resolving this question. His success is beside the point, for when the painter left for Tahiti, he could not be assured that his work would eventually win the world's admiration. Thousands of painters have a faith in their own work that is never shared by history. The opposition here is between moral obligation on the one side and the devotion to art on the other.

We can't argue the merits of the case here (I get to do that elsewhere in my professional life as a philosopher), but we should underscore its relevance to our understanding of making it. True, most of us don't have the intense commitment of Gauguin, nor would our passions result in deserting our families. But whatever the destination we set for ourselves, we better enjoy the journey, because it's on the journey that we spend our lives. We need daydreams in which we see ourselves not just receiving the trophy at the finish line, but enjoying the race as well. Indeed, as you've probably noticed in your own life, having what you want is often less satisfying than getting what you want. Making it in your entrepreneurial career is about the process, not just the product. And failure is failing to try.

Character is crucial

Bad guys sometimes do win. Win, that is, in their professional career, not in their life. Let me tell you about Arthur.

Arthur was always a jerk. He was already an egocentric, nasty kid when we met in first grade, more the psychological bully than a physical tough guy. Although not the brightest kid in the class, he was smart enough to persuade the other kids that everything he excelled at was important and what he was not good at didn't matter. He successfully intimidated his classmates into thinking that by accommodating him, they could ride his coattails to popularity and respect. I always believed, even back in those early years, that when Arthur became an adult, his inconsiderate arrogance would bring him down hard.

Well, schmucks prosper. Not all schmucks, of course, but a lot more than a just world would allow. I met Arthur recently at a wedding, and after massaging a few memories of the old days, we moved on to our current lives. Arthur is an enormously successful real-estate owner, and as he made sure to tell me, made oodles of money in the market during the flush years of the late 1980s. A few minutes of conversation removed any hope that ordinary humility and kindness had somehow infiltrated his personality—the guy was as obnoxious as ever.

It is difficult to accept, though easy to notice, that such character defects are not always an impediment to success in the marketplace. Survey the upper crust of management at your place of work, and you probably will note a few genuinely decent individuals but at least as many horrid ones. In some industries, self-centered coldness regularly trumps warm-hearted fairness, and you may not have to look much further than your own boss for a representative example.

So forget the easy slogans. Nice guys don't always remain on the bottom of the professional ladder, but they don't always reach the top rung either. Honesty doesn't always pay, and caring about others often does siphon your energies away from the progress of your career. But when we take the broader perspective and see our professional activities as just a part of our lives, integrity steers our career decisions. We define ourselves, finally, by our character. Maybe Arthur is happy with who he is, but I'm sure glad I'm not Arthur.

A central theme of this book is that work is crucial to a life well lived, that "just making a living" isn't living enough. So whether your notion of success turns on money, power, status, or admiration, it must also include satisfaction with the work you do. This, too, entails a different sort of daydream. We tend to focus on the benefits of work, not the work itself. But a job well done is not merely a means to other benefits, not a fulfillment of some preordained religious command, not an obligation we have to society, not a test of our skills, but part of the very sinews of how we want our lives to proceed and the values we hold most dear.

The time to take your work and career seriously is now. Not later, when you're married. Not in the future, when you have children. Not in the future, when the children are fully grown. You are already in the middle of your career. You are already responsible for how it's gone so far, and even more responsible for how it goes tomorrow.

Formulating an entrepreneurial career in the new global marketplace is a daunting challenge. Without the safety nets of the traditional workplace, the ability to rebound from frustration and failure will be more important than ever. We will also need the self-assurance to withstand the raised eyebrows and sneers of those who can't pigeonhole our work, who don't understand that we define our careers not by whom we work for but by what we do. And we will need the self-awareness to recognize whether our pursuits truly reflect our personal goals and values.

Do you have the discipline, intellectual honesty, and confidence to succeed in your entrepreneurial career? In the next chapter, we examine what it takes to make sure that you do.

CHAPTER FIVE

What Color Is Your Trampoline?

You are who you are, regardless of who you think you are.

—Oscar Wilde

SUCCESS at work and in one's career have always depended on the fit between one's skills and one's job. In the past, it was rather easy to tell whether that fit was present or absent. Moreover, we didn't worry about making too many wrong decisions at work because from the simplest social rules to major company policies, those decisions were made for us. In the emerging entrepreneurial career, however, self-appraisal will need to be ongoing, and we will be forced to make decisions across the spectrum of our work life.

Without a healthy self-confidence about our choices and decisions, managing the entrepreneurial career is impossible. Self-confidence is an issue only when outcomes are not guaranteed. You don't doubt your ability to count to a hundred, and a lack of self-assurance is not what prevents you from translating Homer from classical Greek to Sanskrit. But as fewer and fewer aspects of the workplace are guaranteed, our self-confidence is under constant challenge and becomes increasingly vulnerable.

Not long ago, to take a commonplace example, dress codes allowed few options and, therefore, little room for mistakes. Now, however, you have decisions to make: Pants or a dress to the company lunch? Is this skirt too short for the meeting with the new client? Suit and tie or casual dress for the sales meeting?

Determining appropriate social relationships at work is also more complicated. Employees and their bosses once shared a tacit recognition of the line between acceptable friendliness and unacceptable fraternizing, but that division is fuzzy in these days of flattened hierarchies. The guidelines for male-female exchanges are even hazier. Just a few years ago, men would act crudely with impunity, but now even the most sensitive men can cross the sexist line. The legal distinction between good-humored banter and harassment is thin to the point of vanishing. Women, for their part, are equally unsure if "acting feminine" is just being who they are or demeaning to their professionalism.

Even more unsettling than the social aspects of the workplace is the nature of work itself. Doubts about one's capacities are never an all-or-nothing, either/or proposition. Notice how the eager salesman down the hall welcomes a difficult account with such bravado but quakes when asked to make a presentation to the boss. One of your associates is as reticent at meetings as the wallpaper behind her but downright stellar when assigned to decipher the most complex financial reports. Take your own internal inventory and you'll come up with a list of tasks that you think you can knock off with an arm tied behind your back and four vodka martinis cruising through your blood-stream, and another list of chores that sends you into glacial dread.

Our apprehensions expand and contract at work as our duties fluctuate with the rapidity and unpredictability of the weather; uncertainty is the constant condition of the modern workplace. Until recently, people went to work expecting to do the same thing they did the day before: gather the hay, place screw number E5 in socket J, make two runs on the bus route, admit patients from 9 A.M. to 5 P.M., install washer-dryers in three homes; tomorrow, they correctly assumed, would be much the same. These days, in contrast, after each executive powwow, entire operating procedures are recast, management introduces some "revolutionary" technology every twenty minutes, and this week's consultant is sure to have suggested yet another revision of the organization's structure. You, of course, are expected to swim with the flow without miss-ing a stroke. Add to this flux the steady erosion of the wall separating your work and private lives, so that just when you think you're in control of your job, you fret that you're failing as a parent (or, if single, you fret about ever finding a spouse and becoming a parent), and when you do concentrate on your home life, you feel guilty about neglecting your career.

No wonder, then, that we're exhausted from the "role overload" of juggling obligations to our parents, our children, our jobs, and ourselves. No wonder, too, that everyone from the CEO to the new temp in the mailroom, to the growing millions working at home, is concerned about having what it takes to manage his or her career.

How can you be confident that the work you do is the right work for you? Are you working hard enough? Too hard? Do your expectations about your career match your talents and the marketplace? To form these and related self-assessments, we need to better understand how we arrive at our self-judgments and how we can so easily be led astray in reaching those judgments.

SIZING YOURSELF UP . . . AND DOWN

Do you think you're sexy? Charming? Wise? Would you describe yourself as witty, responsible, and compassionate? Or would these adjectives suit you better: temperamental, shy, demanding? Do you think you could write a bestselling novel? Are you convinced that you will never master that new computer system in the office or get those projection numbers in on time? We trudge through our lives lugging a full trunk of beliefs about our personality, character, and talents. Some self-assessments remain firm for most of our lives while others are makeshift and soon discarded.

How well do we know ourselves after all? Most of us, most of the time, do get it right. The world has a way of telling us who we are and what we can and cannot do. You don't believe you can fly like Superman even on a dare, and unless you're suffering from institutional-grade pessimism, you don't doubt your capacity to prepare a cup of tea. That said, even sensible people routinely both overestimate and underestimate themselves.

For example, you probably think you look younger than you are—most American adults do. They're convinced they look five years younger than their age and claim to feel about nine years younger. The average American also believes that he or she has better than average health, will live longer than average, and has a better marriage than most other couples. Ninety percent consider themselves better drivers than average. This self-congratulatory pat on the back is already common among teenagers: In a survey of high school students, reported by Thomas Gilgorich in his book *How We Know What Isn't So: The Fallibility of Human Reason in Everyday Life*, nearly all considered themselves average or better when it came to leadership abilities, and a whopping 25 percent considered themselves in the top 1 percent of leaders. In yet another study that helps explain why so many men are clueless about their interpersonal behavior, nine out of ten American men rate their social skills as superior.

When it comes to intellectual abilities, however, confidence levels run the gamut from the highly secure to the highly insecure. Inaccurate assessment of one's intelligence begins early. In one important study, ten thousand students in grades 9–12 were asked to rank their smarts compared with other high school students in the United States.

Of the fifteen hundred in the very lowest-scoring rank, nearly 30 percent believed they were smarter than average, and among this group, nearly 40 percent, believed they were among the very smartest.

Misreading of one's intellectual abilities was no less astonishing in the other direction. Among the top fifteen hundred students, three hundred rated themselves average or below average. In another widely noted study, conducted by psychologist Deborah Philips, 20 percent of early grade school children underestimated their intelligence. Already at this tender age, one in five children suffered from a lack of self-confidence!

We expect people to have their share of skewed interpretations of themselves; we recognize that we have our own set of misconceptions. But occasionally we run into people whose view of themselves is at such variance with reality that we're amazed at how they're able to maintain such distorted beliefs. A therapist friend, Dr. Z, described to me one of his patients who suffered from this syndrome.

"I'm currently treating a stunning young woman we'll call Cindy. Cindy must get complimented on her looks at least ten times a day, and garner a hundred appreciative stares she can't help but notice. Yet, none of this seems to make an impression on her. She discounts all the adulation. 'They're just being polite,' she insists. 'I'm really not that pretty. I've got extra fat on my butt, and this awful pimple on the back of my neck.' Extra fat? Let me tell you, the young lady is an inch from anorexic, and you need an electron microscope to find that pimple. Here is an absolutely gorgeous woman convinced she's average-looking at best. Helping her overcome this negative self-image has not been easy."

We feel bad for people like Cindy. Their insistence on demeaning themselves is perplexing, but we sympathize with their emotional pain. On the other hand, we have little patience with people at the other pole, who are always cocksure about their abilities even when they have no right to be. Unfortunately, these overconfident know-it-alls also have a habit of showing up at our place of work.

Sharon, an assistant buyer at a major New York department store, works for a manager she hates. "If you could peer into my imagination during staff meetings," Sharon says, "you'd agree that I'd make a great murder mystery writer. You'd see the delicious, nasty deaths I invent for that creep. He thinks the title 'supervisor' is a license to supervise every project under way in the universe. No matter what the subject, he knows better than the so-called experts do. This morning, for example, his total ignorance of the facts didn't stop him from delivering a lecture on current trends in sneaker wear in Shanghai to a shoe salesman who just arrived after living in China for two years. He's forever ranting that if he were the CEO, he could turn us into the most lucrative chain in the country. The sick part is that this guy really believes this about himself."

Maintaining an accurate view of yourself

How do people maintain wildly inaccurate views of themselves in the face of a reality that tells them otherwise? For that matter, how do we arrive at accurate views of ourselves? The answer clusters around two psychological approaches to self-evaluation.

We look to our past. In this approach, we base our self-assessment primarily on our personal histories—how we read our past determines how we see ourselves in the present. If asked, say, whether you are organized at work, you'd answer by scanning past projects and judging how well you executed them.

We look to others. According to the second approach, we infer who we are by observing how other people respond to us. In this view, you rate your organizational skills by your employee evaluations and what colleagues say about your work.

These two routes to self-perception are not independent—our memories and our assumptions about other people's opinions feed off one another; nevertheless, one of these two approaches is likely to dominate. Moreover, each of these routes has its own set of nasty psychological traps that impede the struggle to reclaim lost confidence.

Here are a few of the pernicious pitfalls ready to ensnare those who self-evaluate by recollecting the past:

- We accentuate the negative.

Which emotion do you think is stronger—the joy of winning or the pain of losing? The research evidence points overwhelmingly in the direction of woe—losing hurts more than winning feels good. Suffering lingers longer than pleasure. When we win, we raise our sights and quickly move on to the next challenge, but recovery from a loss can take a long time. This explains why you recall in excruciating detail the time you so embarrassed yourself on a date; or perhaps you are among the many who can't shake the memory of a lousy SAT score and remain convinced that you are not good at math. Although, as some evolutionary psychologists conjecture, vivid biological reminders of danger may have served a vital survival function in the earlier lives of our species, focusing on one's mishaps in this era is generally self-destructive. Notice how this inclination stymies Alona.

Alona, a project director at a major insurance company, is in charge of several key pension programs. Her work is demanding and she does it well. The part of her job that makes her most anxious is public speaking. "'Terrified' is a better way to put it," she says. "Usually all I am asked to do is offer introductory remarks at company presentations, but that's enough to induce runaway panic." Alona's colleagues at these functions can't fathom why Alona is so rattled; she may not be a world-class orator, but she manages just fine. Alona, however, is driven by a different memory. At a company retreat several years earlier, she momentarily forgot the name of the senior vice president she was introducing, and when she did remember it, she managed to mangle thoroughly the pronunciation. Alona says she lost it at that point and that the rest of her remarks were a disaster. "That wasn't the first time either," she adds. "I remember screwing up like that in a college speech class."

Alona's unbalanced assessment of herself is an instance of a more general tendency toward bias. We say that seeing is believing, but it is equally true that believing is seeing; we see what we want to see. Psychologists Carol Dweck and Ellen Langer presented a forceful example of how "expectations edit reality."

Suppose you were given the following fragment of a text and told that the author was diagnosed as a schizophrenic.

A Mounted Umbrella

What was the use of not leaving it there where it would hang what was the use if there was no chance of ever seeing it come there and show that it was handsome and right in the way it showed it. The lesson is to learn that it does show it, that it shows it and nothing, that there is nothing, that there is more to do about it and just so much more is there plenty of reason for making an exchange.

After reading the first few strings of words, you probably stopped trying to make sense of the paragraph, concluding that, indeed, it takes a schizophrenic to write such gibberish. You would approach the text with much more respect, however, if you were told beforehand that, as is the case, this was written by the noted author Gertrude Stein. Now you would be more inclined to explain the obscure phrases as a feature of Stein's enigmatic style rather than as an expression of insanity.

When we decide that a person is "good," we describe her behavior in the light of this judgment. Psychologists call this the halo effect. Conversely, when we deem someone "bad," we explain her actions as instances of her badness. We do the same with other traits. Once you've determined that Tim is clumsy, you will explain any future coffee spill by the "fact" that he is awkward; on the other hand, if you don't think Emily is clumsy, her spills are just accidents. We explain our own behavior through the same prism of prejudice: Consider yourself a klutz, and each time you drop something will confirm your "klutzhood," while the other ten thousand times you handle objects flawlessly won't matter in your estimation. And so, too, because Alona has decided that's she is a poor public speaker, she discounts the times she speaks without a glitch but highlights the few inferior outings.

Presumptions about our personal qualities flow in both directions. Speaking before his dramatic bout with Joe Frazier, the supremely confident Muhammad Ali proclaimed, "There's not a man alive who can whup me. I'm too fast. I'm too smart. I'm too pretty. I should be a postage stamp. That's the only way I'll ever get licked." How do such extreme optimists react when they do get licked? The way the eccentric chess virtuoso Bobby Fischer said he would react if he lost his championship match with Boris Spassky: "I'd consider it a fluke," said Fischer.

■ We avoid risks.

Alona's confidence unravels when she gets up to talk, but at least she makes the effort. Others with low self-confidence just run away.

Jeremy has had it with job interviews. "Forget it. I'm no masochist." He's gone through the drill too many times, he says. "I walk into the interview, smile at the secretary, I'm friendly, enthusiastic, knowledgeable, the interview goes well, I smile again at the secretary on the way out, walk out into the street picturing myself sitting in my new office flush with a new title, looking sharp in my new thin-striped, dark-blue suit. I come home feeling exuberant, wait a few anxious days, and then get the letter notifying me that I was a serious contender and they truly enjoyed meeting me, but someone with more suitable experience was hired for the job—and, of course, they sincerely wish me luck in my job search. Dumped again. Who needs this grief?" Jeremy concludes that he can't get a job in this market and stops trying.

This might be a reasonable reaction to a long string of rejection letters, but Jeremy hasn't sent out a résumé to a potential employer in eighteen months, and the four previous rejections he received hardly reflect an overwhelming consensus. Jeremy has been singed but acts like he's been burned. He has become risk-averse.

The professional psychology literature teems with theories that explain how we develop this incapacitating fear of failure. Among the usual suspects are parents and teachers who insisted, despite our natural limitations, that we could succeed at anything if we only tried hard enough. Of course, to everyone's disappointment, we sometimes failed even when we tried very hard. Others emphasize how as adults we impose impossible standards on ourselves. But whatever the cause, the fear of failure is self-reinforcing: You worry that you won't do well, so you don't even try; because you don't try, you can't succeed; and with no inventory of success to draw on, your confidence is further depleted.

Risk aversion is much easier to detect in others than in oneself, and therefore its impact on our career choices is often subtle—but potent. Millions of people, for example, talk endlessly about starting their own business but never manage to put their dream to the test. And what about those computer classes or language classes you've thought of taking? Is it really just time constraints that keep you from enrolling? When our confidence is in the dumps, we're remarkably resourceful at finding ways to evade the risk of failure.

Avoidance is not always an option, however. You're happy to sidestep bothersome tasks, but the world isn't so accommodating. Like it or not, your job comes with responsibilities that you can't elude. In these circumstances, individuals with meager self-confidence turn to a different strategy to preserve their self-worth: sabotage.

■ We self-handicap.

Ulrika is in trouble. She is currently employed as a junior associate at a prestigious investment banking firm in Chicago. For the past several years, Ulrika has been planning to apply to business school and realizes that a positive recommendation from the partners at the company would significantly improve her chances to be accepted at a good business school. Lately, though, she's having second thoughts about her aptitude for this profession. Her recent work has been mediocre at best, certainly not of the caliber that elicits first-rate recommendations. Ulrika is, in fact, self-destructing. One day last week she was expected to submit an important portfolio analysis. She partied until the wee hours the night before, telling herself as she boogied on the dance floor that she'd be able to wing it the next day. She arrived at the office late, hungover, and exhausted, and submitted a dreadful presentation.

Self-handicapping is seductive. The lure is a seeming win-win alternative. You set yourself up for failure so that if indeed you do poorly, you can blame your shoddy performance on external impediments rather than on inability. On the other hand, if you happen to do well, then wow!—you're so capable that you succeed despite the obstacles. Usually, the ploy is easily recognized. Haven't you taken an exam after deliberately and perversely spending the previous night gossiping or watching old movies instead of studying? But self-handicapping can also operate just below the conscious level: Sometimes we are only dimly aware of how determined we are to get ourselves into trouble when, for example, we hand in assignments late or postpone important phone calls. The lesson is to make certain that in planning your career, you haven't half-consciously built in the seeds of its destruction with ready-made excuses for quitting.

Another set of traps that distort accurate self-assessment lie in ambush along the second route to self-evaluation—seeing yourself as you think other people see you.

Stop! Don't change that dial! When people hear the words "as other people see you," they immediately raise their palms in the air, shake their heads, and righteously intone, "Not me. I don't care what other people think. I always do my own thing, follow my own standards, march to my own drummer, follow my own star." Listen, if you truly didn't ever care what other people thought, you'd be reading this book in the locked reading room of the local mental hospital. But because you're sane and recognize that you live with other human beings, you don't wear a toga to work or a loincloth to the supermarket, no matter how comfortable you find those styles. You think in a shared language, not in your own private jabber. You have sufficient civility not to blare "Mary Had a Little Lamb" on a tuba in the middle of the street in the middle of the night, and hopefully you finally stopped inflicting your Bill Clinton impersonation on accommodating friends.

In fact, most human attributes are comparative descriptions. A short Watusi is a giant to a Pygmy. Alone in the world, you can't be rich or poor, kind or nasty, charming or dull, an incorrigible slob or compulsively neat, a loyal friend or an unreliable creep. To the woman who informed me without a smidgen of embarrassment that she considers herself drop-dead gorgeous but that no one else has the refined taste to recognize her beauty, I'm sorry to say that it's social consensus, not individual opinion, that determines attractiveness. (What I did say, passive-aggressive coward that I am, was that perhaps people didn't notice her beauty because they didn't want to "drop dead.") We can dispute the extent to which our attributes are formed by the culture we live in, the degree to which we are "social constructions," in the jargon of social theory, but incontrovertibly, much of how we think of ourselves is a reflection of how we think others think of us; we are individuals not despite culture but because of culture.

For the most part, we do a pretty good job of estimating how we appear to other people. Those who don't are easily recognizable. We are all too familiar, for example, with the perversely thickheaded jerk who is so convinced of his charm that he's oblivious to the tedium he evokes in everyone else. Conversely, when your self-regard is in the basement, you misjudge the consensus people have of you and accept the negative opinions of one or two individuals. The marvelous physical therapist who treated my basketball knee injury was uniformly admired by all her colleagues in the clinic, but thought of herself as second-rate because she hadn't earned the respect of her supervisor.

Indeed, the "significant other," the person whose opinion counts most with us need not even be alive. For Richard, that person was Uncle Red. Richard recalls a painful conversation he had when he was sixteen. He told his uncle of his hope to someday start his own business. Uncle Red shook his head and said, "You are a talented young man, Richard, but I'm afraid you don't have a head for business." Over the years, Richard has toyed with the idea of opening his own electronics store, but each time he sets himself to make the move, Uncle Red's comment lights up like a neon sign in his head, and he doesn't take the plunge. The impact of Uncle Red's comments hasn't waned even though he's been dead for ten years.

But why do we have these fixations? Why would anyone who thinks poorly of herself seek relationships with people who reinforce this lack of confidence? Isn't it demeaning to be with people who think you're a loser?

■ We self-validate . . . even at our own expense.

You're at a restaurant and observe this scenario unfold like a piece of public theater. At the table next to you a man berates a woman who, you surmise, is his wife. "You're an utter fool," he bellows, either oblivious to the people around him or just not caring what they think. "You actually paid a hundred dollars for that piece of shit? Are you really that stupid?" he screams. The sarcasm and rebukes go on throughout the meal. You don't understand why this woman stands for the humiliation, why she just doesn't get up and leave the restaurant and her obnoxious husband.

William Swann, Professor of Psychology at Ohio University, wondered, too. Determined to gain a deeper understanding of this behavior, he undertook a decades-long research project into why people acquiesce in this ridicule. One plausible path proved to go nowhere: Abused spouses were not masochists who secretly enjoyed the denigration. What Swann and his associates discovered pointed to a different intuition: We have a powerful need to have other people confirm what we believe about ourselves. We go about our lives, make our plans, and form relationships on the basis of how we think we appear to others. Challenges to those assumptions can be extremely threatening. In the terminology of famed psychoanalyst Heinz Kohut, when our desire for self-validation or "mirroring" is frustrated, the self-concept begins to fragment, causing a sinking feeling that something is terribly wrong. We go to great lengths to make sure this doesn't happen—think of the boss who can't handle anyone challenging his dominance, so he surrounds himself only with "yes men."

People with low self-confidence are willing, therefore, to abide the derision of persons close to them in exchange for the comfort of having their tarnished self-image affirmed. This explains, at least in part, why people remain at jobs where they are constantly belittled. Take Terry, for example. She doesn't think much of her abilities. Her boss doesn't either, and tells her so regularly. Terry comes home to her ego-busting husband, who joins the chorus. "Honey, I'm sorry the boss chewed you out today, but let's face it, he has a point." Terry feels awful, but at least her judgment of herself is corroborated.

We humans are also remarkably adept at getting people to see us as we see ourselves. James Coyne, University of Michigan psychologist, observed the well-honed strategies depressed individuals use to induce unsuspecting strangers to dislike them. They can achieve this result with even a brief telephone conversation; and so, too, people who lack confidence almost guarantee that others won't have confidence in them. Notice, for example, how they regularly begin expressing their opinion with caveats such as "You might think I'm dumb for saying this, but . . ." or how they systematically avoid eye contact.

Self-images are formed in a complex series of facing mirrors. We decide who we are on the basis of how we think we appear to others and then make sure that others see us that way, thereby reinforcing our initial judgment.

■ We deflect compliments.

How do you maintain low self-confidence when everyone around you tells you how terrific you are? You refuse to believe them.

Researchers find that even those of us with healthy self-confidence enjoy praise in moderation but are uncomfortable when the adulation becomes shamelessly enthusiastic. Accepting acclaim is, of course, even more difficult when your pride is meager. "You have a wonderful sense of humor," someone says to you, and you think he's just being polite; she says, "Your baby is so cute," and your internal response is "That's what they say about all babies"; your boss thanks you for your help on the project, and you see this as just routine management talk. Successful people who think of themselves as impostors, apparently a fairly common phenomenon, regularly downgrade all compliments as phony and upgrade all criticisms as sincere.

SUSTAINING SELF-CONFIDENCE IN THE NEW WORK ENVIRONMENT

It's never too late to be what you might have been.
—George Eliot

We fool ourselves about lots of things, but self-deception is rife when it comes to dealing with our confidence. We set ourselves up to be self-duped. As we've seen, a host of psychological habits—including self-handicapping, risk aversion, deflecting positive assessments, an emphasis on the negative, and a constant need to self-validate—can readily distort one's self-appraisal. This brings to mind the story of the judge who asks the thief, "Don't you feel awful stealing from people who gave you their trust?" The thief answers, "But it's very difficult to steal from people if they don't trust you." The con artist—the confidence man, as he was called—is a swindler who gains your trust in order to take advantage of you. But we can con ourselves, too. We do that, for example, by unjustly convincing ourselves that we don't have what it takes to succeed.

Self-critical judgments are especially tempting in the new global marketplace, where one's abilities are untested and past achievements are quickly obsolete. In this new marketplace, self-confidence is easily lost and difficult to regain. That's because, to make the effort, you need to scrape together all the self-confidence you have remaining. Indeed, renewing and maintaining self-confidence in one's ability to manage the entrepreneurial-career will engage one's complete resolve and intellectual honesty.

The following are a few observations to help us on our way.

Minver Cheevy born too late
Scratched his head and kept on thinking;

Miniver coughed and called it fate
And kept on drinking.

—Edward Arlington Robinson

Recognize your limitations

Back in the late 1960s, one of the "instant insights" that Americans loved to pin on their walls urged us to worry about what we could change, not to worry about what we couldn't change, and to have the wisdom to know the difference. By all indications, we're not very wise. We persist in trying to change what we cannot, and blame external forces for preventing us from changing what, in fact, we could change. These are costly mistakes: Americans annually spend billions of dollars and billions of hours trying to improve their bodies, their personalities, and their skills. A few of these ventures work, most don't, and a few are downright counterproductive.

Because we steadfastly believe in free will, certain that we are the masters of our fate, we are loath to acknowledge our innate personal limitations. We preach: "Try hard, and you can be anyone and do anything you want." We certainly ought not to foreclose goals too early, but at some point unqualified encouragement turns into a cruel lie. "Hope," Francis Bacon wisely observed, "is a good breakfast but a bad supper." If you are tone-deaf, ten thousand voice lessons won't be enough to get you the title role of Aida at the Metropolitan Opera. And, sorry, but don't expect to take home the Wimbledon trophy if you

167

were thirty years old when you had your first tennis lesson. Not everyone can do everything, and you only set up your confidence for a fall if you believe otherwise.

In the past few years we've discovered that many of these limitations are hereditary and impervious to our choices. With regard to health, for example, inheritors of Huntington's disease have an overlong CAG repeat near the tip of chromosome 4 and, at present, will develop the disease no matter how they live. In other cases, the hereditary influence is substantial if not decisive. We've learned that schizophrenia isn't caused by bad parenting or curable by talk therapy, but is substantially dependent on one's genes. We now know that the reason why Jack but not Joe is an alcoholic, even though they are equally attracted to booze, depends to some extent on their inherited endowments, and that the reason nearly all diets fail is that one's weight hovers around a preset plateau, and it takes a Herculean effort to permanently shift from that set point. At this juncture in our remedial skills, we can cure most phobias and help sexual dysfunction, but are utterly incapable of altering a person's sexual preference.

Not only do we blame ourselves when we shouldn't, we also illegitimately take credit when we don't deserve it and refuse blame when we do deserve it. Seasoned casino gamblers and young Wall Street broncos alike attribute their winnings to their clever calculations but their losses to a run of bad luck. Misunderstanding the cause-and-effect relationship, we automatically trace adult misbehavior to a troubled childhood. It is true, for example, that victims of abuse are six times more likely to abuse their own children, but 70 percent of abused children do not become abusive parents. No doubt, the most likely scapegoats of all for one's troubles are other people: Husbands blame their wives, wives blame their husbands, both blame their marriage; employees blame their managers, managers blame their employees, and both blame "the system."

Like the little engine that believed it could, persuading yourself that you can climb the mountain gets you to try, and when you succeed, your confidence is nourished even more. Without some faith in yourself, you won't undertake a new business venture or learn a new skill at work, and never discover that you had these talents. But unchecked self-confidence, remember, isn't always a good idea. Sometimes you can fail only once—as did the fellow who thought he could jump out of a plane and fly—but you also can persevere in attempts to do that for which you simply have no talent. In those cases, each defeat further erodes resolve.

Respect the power of self-fulfilling prophecies

Most of the interesting challenges we face at work and in our personal lives aren't either sure winners or sure losers (otherwise, of course, they wouldn't be interesting challenges). In these uncertain circumstances, our attitudes make a crucial difference. According to Einstein's general theory of relativity, the mass of an object changes the shape of the space around it, and analogously, whether you see human ability as fluid and open to change, or as rigid and immutable, alters the probability of succeeding at some task. Researching this phenomenon, Carol Taylor found that when students of similar abilities did poorly on tests, those who viewed intelligence as a fixed quality tended to be discouraged and gave up, while those who saw intelligence as dynamic and capable of improvement remained upbeat in the face of setbacks and improved. This finding is in accord with an important body of research on "learned helplessness" pioneered by Martin Seligman. In psych jargon, the learned helplessness hypothesis posits that "uncontrollable coercive stimulation results in generalized motivational deficits"—translated into English, this means that if you expose individuals to conditions in which they believe they have no control and then measure how they do on subsequent tasks, you find them doing more poorly than they would do otherwise. Convinced that you're stupid, you won't try to learn.

Seligman discovered evidence for this phenomenon in his early experiments with dogs. He observed that when the animals were repeatedly shocked but could do nothing to prevent the jolt, they remained passive even later when they could have escaped the shock with just a slight effort. The dogs had become victims of "learned helplessness." Seligman found the same pattern of behavior in people who had convinced themselves that their lack of ability was permanent. The "learned hopeful" view defeats as merely momentary setbacks that do not reflect their true abilities, but the "learned helpless" internalize failure and respond, "See, I'm stupid." After a tough day at work, the hopeful think, "The boss is in a foul mood today," but the helpless conclude, "Forget it, the boss is a bastard."

An intriguing related experiment in the workplace also demonstrates the effect of one's beliefs on one's self-image. Employees who received a bad evaluation were quicker to leave a room that had large mirrors than were employees who received a positive evaluation, and more quickly than employees with the same poor evaluation who were in a room without mirrors. Moreover, those who were led to believe that they could improve their performance were more inclined to remain in the mirrored room than those who thought their evaluation reflected an unalterable inability.

It's the standard pep talk, but a needed one: To play is sometimes to lose, but it's the possibility of defeat that makes the victories sweet. You can hit a home run only if you're willing to fail in the attempt—Babe Ruth struck out thirteen hundred times. Sam Walton, the billionaire founder of Wal-Mart, made this point concisely in this snippet from an interview with him:

Q: Mr. Walton, what was the secret to your success?
A: Right decisions.
Q: And how did you manage to make these right decisions?
A: Experiences.
Q: Yes, and how did you come to your experiences?
A: Bad decisions.

Self-confident optimists are willing to try and try again, but not because they are better at predicting the future than self-doubting pessimists. In fact, optimists are worse at predictions! Repeated studies confirm that people in states of depression (a psychological profile related to pessimism) are less likely to underestimate risks or overestimate the likelihood of a positive outcome in games of chance, and are more accurate in assessing their social skills. The deceptions of optimism are, however, necessary to get by in life.

Anthropologist Lionel Tiger argues in *Optimism: The Biology of Hope* that optimism is a natural human condition and that "Our benign sense of the future could have been bred into us and other complex animals out of the need to survive." If our ancestors were cool calculators who always carefully weighed the odds before conducting the hunt or undertaking some other questionable mission, they wouldn't have had descendants to write about them. Survival, Tiger speculates, is dependent on a willingness to take risks, and risks depend on hopes that aren't always justified by past experience. As a character in Ibsen's play *The Wild Duck* says, "Take away the life-lie from the average person and you take away his happiness along with it."

Self-confidence, however, is not merely idle hope; the very decision to try some activity alters your brain. When you undertake a project, you mentally rehearse the upcoming activity—the plan of action, the response of others, the potential hurdles and how you will overcome them, the joys of vindication—and all this activity affects one's neuroanatomy. Dr. Stephen Lisberger, a neuroscientist at the University of California, San Francisco, has studied this phenomenon in depth and explains in a report on his work in the *Wall Street Journal* that "the same cell networks involved in executing a task are also involved in imagining it." For example, identical brain configurations are found in people who play a piece of music in their mind's eye as in people who actually practice it.

Mental preparation helps, but we ought not to forget that significant improvement comes only with actual practice. The primary reason modern athletes are much better than those of earlier generations is that they begin training at an earlier age and continue to train longer and harder; the gold medal marathon winner at the 1904 Olympics would not even qualify to run in today's Boston Marathon. And while practice doesn't necessarily make perfect or even get you to Carnegie Hall, it can overturn even your most hardened assumptions about your lack of talent.

Researchers at Carnegie Mellon University provided a dramatic example of how practice affects even mental performance. The average person can store seven digits in short-term memory. These researchers were able to teach college students to memorize much longer strings of digits, so that after fifty hours of practice with different numbers, four students were able to recall more than twenty digits after a single hearing. One student, not especially gifted in math, was able to recall an astounding 102 digits. But it took him four hundred hours of practice to achieve this feat.

Repeated failures might be telling you something about your overblown expectations, but we've also seen that when the goal is realistic, the willingness to make an attempt increases the chance for success. And nothing breeds confidence like success.

Self-esteem is earned, not given

> *No one can make you feel inadequate without your permission.*
>
> —Eleanor Roosevelt

It hasn't been easy, but I've deliberately avoided using the term "self-esteem" throughout this discussion of self-confidence. Not only is the term as vague and overused as "spirituality" or "empowerment," it is also self-defeating. All this talk about self-esteem is helping to destroy our self-esteem.

In the 1980s, the self-esteem movement swept across the country. The racks of every kiosk in the country sported half a dozen magazines with lead stories on how to increase your self-esteem and thereby find a lover, become a better lover, or keep up your spirits when your lover leaves you. Improved self-esteem was propounded as the necessary ingredient to making more money and better relationships, while low self-esteem was denounced as the cause of social ills stretching from addiction to fear of intimacy to suicide. Diminished self-esteem was implicated as the cause of poor learning in children. An appealing theory . . . except that it isn't true.

Let's dispense with the obvious. As we emphasized earlier, how you feel about yourself affects how well you do. People with little self-esteem, who don't regard themselves as lovable and competent, aren't likely to accomplish great things. The downside of self-esteem, however, kicks in when we insist on lauding ourselves and others even when we don't deserve the applause. Low self-esteem, it turns out, is typically a result of poor performance rather than its cause. Roy Baumeister, one of the nation's leading researchers in the study of self-esteem, explains in an article in the *Journal of Personality and Social Psychology* how people who mess up their lives end up with lowered self-worth: "When the destructive consequences of self-regulation failure catch up with them and they contemplate the sorry state of their lives, they feel a loss of self-esteem. As a result, they come to associate the problem with the loss of self-esteem—but conclude wrongly that the low self-esteem is the cause rather than the result of reckless or self-destructive behavior." In other words, having low self-esteem doesn't make you an alcoholic, but being an alcoholic destroys your self-esteem.

Part of the appeal of explaining dysfunction in terms of weak self-esteem is tied to our habit of "psychologizing" all behaviors—we're reluctant to admit that sometimes what you see is what's really there. Bullies and conceited jerks, we want to believe, really suffer from inferiority complexes. But the most careful studies make clear that gang leaders and criminals often have as much self-esteem as any overachievers, and their bluster comes from arrogance, not from underdeveloped self-esteem. (Indeed, when their inflated self-esteem is challenged by reality, they feel "dissed," and often turn violent.)

Here's the point. If you're feeling downcast about yourself, it's likely connected to your underachieving. And you won't win back your confidence with feel-good proclamations about what a wonderful person you are. Reminding yourself to take pride in how well you do watercolors won't give you the resolve you need to take on the new and difficult marketing project they've assigned to you. We condescend when we try to boost the self-esteem of others with unearned or irrelevant praise, and we can condescend to ourselves the same way. Notice, too, that we patronize only those we don't respect. Genuine self-respect promotes self-confidence but precludes false self-esteem. You'll improve your self-esteem when you improve your life.

RELYING ON YOUR STANDARDS, YOUR VALUES, YOUR INTEGRITY

Self-confidence means, finally, that you're willing to confide in yourself. But that entails having a good assessment of yourself.

We evaluate ourselves, as we saw, both through internal memories and by considering how we seem to others. Each method is a check and balance against the other. We all seek to impress those around us: We replace our clothes with fashionable new ones, we go hungry to make ourselves suitably thin, we read books and articles that make us seem smart, we rehearse for our turn in a conversation, and we adopt physical and speaking mannerisms to distinguish ourselves from the crowd. You cannot, in truth, determine your strengths and weaknesses without referring to the opinions of other people, but your confidence will never be secure if your self-image is totally dependent on others. At the same time, we also noted the dangers of depending exclusively on your own impressions in determining your qualities and defects: Memories are flawed, and judgments are rife with biases and expectations.

Productive self-confidence, in summary, demands an appreciation of what you can and cannot achieve, bolstered by a determination to make the attempt even when the odds are less than promising. It requires a consideration of other people's judgments and, most important, an inner core of independence and intellectual honesty.

That spirit of independent and honest thinking is the hallmark of the successful career-entrepreneur. Having the self-confidence to accept responsibility for one's career now must include the self-confidence to accept the values and standards that propel that career.

When you value your work, excuses for not working dissipate. Procrastination, for example, is recognized for the irresponsibility it is, and the psychological explanations for its grip on us are no longer a defensible justification for avoiding our work. Work that violates your integrity poses less of a temptation, even when the pay is substantial. And when your standards of evidence are high, you are less likely to embark on dead-end ventures that enjoy the passing popularity of the crowd but make little sense in the long run. If these seem like noble aspirations for a life and not

just a career, this is precisely the point. In the entrepreneurial career, one's personal life and one's work form a
seamless whole, and self-confidence must address all of
that life.

We need this self-confidence in our leisure as well. As
the best work is creative and self-motivated, so, too, the
best leisure is creative and self-motivated. Leisure thrives,
as does our career, when we bring to it self-confidence,
independent thinking, and the integrity of our values.

CHAPTER SIX

Creating a Leisure Ethic

What can we say about those millions of people whose life's ambition is to rest when not tired, whose utopian ideal is a blank strip of white sand where they may slowly oxidize in an endless spell of fair weather?

—Robert Grodin

. . . What is a man,
If his chief good and market of his time
Be but to sleep and feed?

—Hamlet, 4.4

Leisure and free time live in two different worlds. We have gotten into the habit of thinking they are the same. Anybody can have free time. Not everyone can have leisure.

—Sebastian de Graza

S UNDAY morning. Eileen has finished her coffee. She's read most of the paper, put aside the magazine section. There's an article in it she hopes to get to later, though, as usual, she probably never will. So, what to do today?

Eileen calls her friend Jody. Jody's not home. A bummer. Now what? She could organize cabinets, but who wants to spend Sunday rearranging dishes and half-used boxes of pasta? Maybe she'll take in a movie. The new Woody Allen film? Think not; he's beginning to get on her nerves. Mildly bored, she flicks on the TV. A show about the south of France captures her attention for a few minutes, and then, after some thumb shopping on the remote, she alights on an old Cary Grant flick with . . . whatshername . . . Doris Day? Hours go by. Jody calls. They talk for a chunk about Ross, the new man in Jody's life. Should she dump him, Jody wants to know. Eileen thinks, yes, maybe that makes sense. Later, Eileen chats with her mother, and they argue about why Eileen won't visit this week. She hangs up and takes an overdue trip to the supermarket—the milk is sour—and then it's back home for more television. Voilà, it's evening.

"Where the hell did the day go?" Eileen wonders. This was supposed to be her day off. So why does she feel so empty and restless, so vaguely depressed?

Eileen's hollow day is a good example of a bad problem: We are in desperate need of a leisure ethic. We work hard and productively, but we leisure terribly. That's not so surprising: Doing leisure well is more difficult than working well. Work, after all, presents you with concrete tasks, but the demands of leisure are of your own making. Work brings you tangible rewards when you do it proficiently and penalties when you do it poorly, but the rewards of leisure are more subtle and private (indeed, some say that, by definition, if you get paid for doing something, it isn't leisure). You can easily spend an entire life in shallow, unfulfilling leisure. Many do.

But at a price. Neglected leisure contaminates all the corners of one's life. When your leisure is anemic, you can't have a healthy sense of humor about yourself; that's why people who don't know how to play are such sourpusses. Uninspired leisure also infects your work life and turns it into a ceaseless drag.

The impact of leisure on our work will matter even more in the future. In the new world of open employment where we do jobs, not have them, work life and personal life merge. Work time will be "on your own time," to waste, conserve, or spend. Time management will no longer be just a seminar topic offering tips for improving efficiency, but an essential issue in our lives. Because you can work all the time if you so choose, you can also feel guilty all the time you don't. Conversely, you can decide to work hardly at all and continuously blame it on "pressing personal demands." At the center of time management, therefore, is the management of your leisure.

AT YOUR LEISURE: A WORKING DEFINITION

Do you remember filling out forms that asked you to name your hobbies? Hobbies are history—the word is nearly as quaint as the hobby shops of the past. What do people do instead? Mostly, they watch television.

But viewing reruns of *Seinfeld* is not leisure, any more

than is doing the laundry, preparing your tax return, or visiting sick relatives. Leisure isn't simply time spent not working. Nor should leisure be confused with rest: Leisure is no more about relaxing than work is about relaxing. Leisure is not about diversion either. It is purposeful, focused activity. You could be enjoying your leisure while praying in church, listening to Mozart, making love, hanging out with friends, or fixing a broken drain pipe. When was the last time you took a long walk by yourself to be by yourself? That's genuine leisure, too.

Work is directed to external creativity; leisure is directed to internal creativity. The object of leisure's re-creation is our own spirit. When we work effectively, our production enhances the world, and when our leisure is productive, we nourish ourselves. In the terminology of our biblical tradition, leisure is the creative Sabbath of our creative work.

The ancient Greeks thought of leisure as time devoted to self-nourishment. The word for leisure in classical Greek is *scole* (school), and the word for work is *ascholia* (not-leisure); similarly, the Latin word for leisure is *otium* (schooling), and for work is *negotium* (not-leisure). In this hierarchy, work is the absence of leisure, not the other way around: "We work," says Aristotle, "in order to have leisure." The Athenian ideal was to free citizens from daily physical toil so that they could engage in leisure uses of the mind, such as listening to music, learning, and contemplation, along with civic participation.

The theory behind these priorities is that true gratification comes only from doing something for its own sake. Therefore, working for someone else can never produce happiness. For the same reason, resting to regain your strength for more labor can't provide authentic satisfaction either. In contrast, says Aristotle, leisure offers "intrinsic pleasure, intrinsic happiness, intrinsic felicity."

We do not share the disdain for work of this ancient elite—an attitude they could afford, by the way, since in both ancient Greece and ancient Rome, slaves did all the physical work. But we should reacquaint ourselves with their understanding of leisure as an indispensable activity, not merely a passive passing of time. Work and leisure are complementary. And just as work is at its best when it has intrinsic value, so leisure is most satisfying when it is not a means but an end in itself.

THE TIME OF YOUR LIFE

Squandered leisure is a significant social problem. Millennia ago, Aristotle pointed to Sparta as an example of what happens when a society cannot master its leisure. The tough city-state, run like a military garrison, defeated democratic Athens in the Peloponnesian War but collapsed in the peace that followed. Echoing that warning, the illustrious twentieth-century philosopher Bertrand Russell argued that the final test of a civilization is the ability to use leisure wisely. Russell didn't think we were doing well in that regard. He was right.

Collectively, we waste so much of our precious leisure time. But how are we doing individually? Are you content with the way you spend your discretionary time?

"What discretionary time?" you say. Like most Americans, you probably see yourself galloping through life at breakneck speed, barely finding the time to catch your breath, and here you're being lectured on how to improve your leisure time. I got an earful of this reaction from Brenda, an events planner at a large corporation.

"Leisure? Are you kidding? Let me tell you my schedule, okay? Ten-hour workdays are typical, though in the past few insane months, there have been plenty of twelve-hour days, too. So when I come home from a draining day at the office, my desires are simple. I want to kick off my shoes, luxuriate on occasion with a glass of wine, and then space out in front of the television set. It's lovely to hear all about leisure as self-improvement, but the last thing I want to do when I come home is conjugate French verbs."

Brenda has this much right: Leisure is not about "bettering oneself." It is about enjoying yourself. And that moves us on to the next critical question: How do you bring joy to your self? It is astonishing how we neglect to pinpoint the activities that give us pleasure. Like Brenda, we avoid the question by insisting that we don't have the time to do the things that we'd like. So the first step in reclaiming leisure is to review how much free time we have at our disposal, how wisely we've been using that time, and why we usually feel rushed.

Americans love to quantify. We have statistics for everything: the tonnage of salsa eaten each winter, the number of tourists visiting Savannah each summer, the amount of money teenagers spend annually on jeans, the record for strikeouts pitched by a southpaw on a July 12 when the sky is overcast, and even the number of Elizabeth Taylor's husbands. Of late, driven in large part by marketing interests, a torrent of surveys has examined how Americans spend their time at work and at home. The details can get pretty detailed. For example, I can report to you that on an average day, Americans spend 54 million dollars on toys; eat the equivalent of 2,250 cattle at McDonalds, 75 acres' worth of pizza, and 3 million gallons of ice cream; drink 1.2 million gallons of hard liquor and enough cans of beer to fill a baseball stadium 30 feet deep. We read more on Wednesdays and Thursdays than on Monday and Tuesdays, and socialize most on Sundays.

All statistical surveys are suspect, of course (or should we say 8.3 out of 10 surveys are suspect?), but reports on how we allocate our time are especially dubious. For one thing, the conclusions of these studies regularly contradict one another. Adding to the confusion is the variety of definitions used by these polls. Do "hours at work" include your time drinking coffee down the hall? How about the time you spend, while in the office, talking to your child on the phone? Does free time include the hours you shop for groceries and prepare dinner? Are you using leisure time when you bring your car in for a tune-up? There is no uniformly accepted answer.

The most serious problem with these time studies, however, is our own self-deception. People's accounts of time use are notoriously unreliable. We deceive the pollsters and ourselves about the number of hours we actually work (we tend to overestimate the time); how much time we spend sleeping (we sleep more than we think we do); how much time we spend reading (we read less than we say); and how much time we spend watching television (we watch more than we admit). We also don't do much of what we say we like to do. When asked for their favorite activity, people say their number one choice is "having sex." Yet the average time reported for making love is twenty-two minutes a week, considerably less than the time spent on financial planning!

After clearing away the mist formed by these conflicting studies and the mass of unverified and deceptive self-reports, and relying on the best of recent research, two conclusions emerge about our free time. In combination, they pose a conundrum:

- We work fewer hours than we did in the recent past.

- We feel more rushed than we did in the recent past.

What's going on? Why the disconnection between perception and reality? This is a societywide phenomenon that might well be true of you: Do you have more free time but feel more harried anyway? An examination of the reason for this seeming inconsistency will point the way to a healthier leisure.

Unquestionably, Americans work hard. And unquestionably, this is our choice. Biology certainly doesn't mandate that we put in those long hours. The book of

Proverbs suggests, "Go to the ant, thou sluggard; consider her ways and be wise," but ants don't scurry about when they aren't hunting for food or escaping predators. Those supposedly restless creatures, the busy bees and beavers, spend only a small fraction of their time being busy—we just happen to notice them when they are. Animals mostly hang out.

Full-time work isn't natural to humans either. In fact, our ancestors worked fewer days than we do. The Athenians celebrated between fifty and sixty holidays a year, and the Romans over a hundred. Our image of feudal serfs breaking their backs tilling their lords' fields is soothed by noting that the Christian Middle Ages observed 115 holidays a year—add 50 Sundays, and that comes to around 3 days of vacation a week. You'd work much less even today were you a member of the Kapakus of Papau, who work one day and rest the next, or Australian Aborigines, who work for only several hours a day and only four days a week.

Americans, on average, work more than most people on the planet, including their economic counterparts in Europe. French and English workers, for example, get twenty-two working days of holiday, and Germans even more, while the average American gets no more then ten days.

Reflecting this national industriousness, Americans say they feel constantly rushed. According to a poll conducted by the *Wall Street Journal* and WNBC in 1996, 20 percent of us feel hurried to the point of discomfort. Having money doesn't help. Three-quarters of the people who made more than a hundred thousand dollars a year said that managing their time was a bigger problem for them than managing their money. In another survey, when asked if they considered themselves workaholics, a third of the fathers said yes, a fifth of the mothers said yes, and a third of the people said their partners were workaholics. And though many studies suggest that most Americans wouldn't want to reduce their workweek and most say they enjoy their jobs, they complain, nonetheless, about having too little time to do what they'd like.

We are people in a hurry. We no longer bother with frozen juice concentrates but buy premixed juice in containers. Dogs are losing in popularity to the less dependent, less time-intensive cats. Old-fashioned "snail mail" is too slow for the growing ranks of E-mail users. We are impatient when a software application takes more than a few seconds to boot. Seven percent of the respondents in the *Wall Street Journal* survey noted above, consider daydreaming a waste of time. We would assume that this upsurge in haste and time pressure is the result of steadily decreasing amounts of disposable time. But we'd assume incorrectly. True, we work hard, harder than most, but we also work less than we did in decades past.

Although some social scientists, such as Juliet Schor in *The Overworked American*, have argued that Americans spend more time at the office now than ever, others conclude the opposite: that Americans in fact gained one hour per day of free time from 1965 to 1985 and that this seven hours per week decrease has held steady since. (Men have reduced their work time even more than women, but those with more education gained fewer free hours than those with less education.) This reduction is a result, in part, of our entering the workforce at a later age and retiring earlier. Americans also have more free time than before because, on average, they marry later, have fewer children, and spend considerably less time doing housework. But if we are, in fact, working less than before, why does it feel more hectic than ever? A number of factors are to blame.

One factor is the quicker tempo and increased responsibilities on the job. We interpret our fatigue as resulting not only from working harder but also from working longer. We also underestimate the duration of our free time because it now comes in smaller packets and is scattered primarily over the weekends—we enjoy fewer large blocks of discretionary hours. Another factor that some consider key to understanding our sense of time pressure is that we live through more transformations in our lives than our parents did. We more frequently change jobs, partners, and homes, and these shifts heighten the sense of time being compressed.

In their comprehensive study *Time for Life: The Surprising Ways Americans Use Their Time*, John P. Robinson and Geoffrey Godbey trace our feelings of time overload to a pervasive misunderstanding and dysfunctional use of leisure. We have adopted, these authors say, an "expanding sense of necessity," constantly adding to our list of things we think we absolutely must have or do. Our free time is expanding, but not as fast as this catalog of needs. You're bound to feel time-deprived if you treat leisure as another obligation, into which you have to cram as much as possible . . . a tennis lesson, conversations with friends, a movie, a gourmet dinner, that television show, an aerobics class. Leisure is now measured in terms of efficiency, and consequently we neglect our need for tranquility. We forget to enjoy what we're doing.

So the first step in recovering leisure time is to reassert control over your free time. No more the victim mentality that throws up its hands and proclaims, "Modern life has robbed me of my free time, and I can do nothing about it." Of course you can do something about it. Indeed, as the line between making a living and making a life becomes increasingly thin, it is even more imperative that you reconfigure your free time.

Think of it this way. Besides the hours you spend at work, getting there and coming home; dealing with food, family obligations, social necessities widely construed; and, if you're among the virtuous, some exercise, how much free time do you actually have? The average American has about forty hours of discretionary time a week. Does this seem too high a number in your case? Halve it. You still have plenty of time. And so, again, how do you spend your noncaptive hours?

If you are like most Americans, the answer is "watching television." We can't afford to be overly delicate— no serious discussion of leisure can treat television viewing as an aside. Not only is sitting in front of the tube number one on the list of the top ten ways we spend our free time, but it exceeds all the other activities combined. You might be an exception (you are atypical—after all, you read, and you even read nonfiction), but even those of us who watch less television than average, watch more than we should. And if too much television is not a problem for you, it probably is for someone in your home. Whoever tells most of the stories to most of the people most of the time assumes the cultural role of parent and school. Television now tells our stories.

Prolonged television watching is the antithesis of robust leisure. The time television steals from other leisure activities is just one of its harmful consequences; television also impairs physical fitness and depletes social life. Watching lots of television affects our moods—you know that crummy feeling after wasting three hours staring at the box. To appreciate the scale of the problem, let's visit the all-American home of John and Clarissa.

Scene I. Fade In. Interior. Living room, evening.

John is sitting in his E-Z chair, a magazine resting on his lap. Clarissa is on the couch next to him. On the wall at their backs is a clock sporting a boat motif. It reads 8:20 P.M. The light in the room is low and flickering. John and Clarissa are watching television.

John has been watching television all his life. He is unusual in having had a television set when he grew up in the early 1950s, when less than 10 percent of the population had TVs. Now, 98 percent of homes have television sets—more than have refrigerators or indoor plumbing. John and Clarisa have four sets. In addition to the one they are watching, there is one in their bedroom, one in the room of their teenage daughter, Vicky, and just last month they bought a set for little Pete. Four television sets is not unusual. The majority of American homes now have at least three: 32 percent of six-to-seven-year-olds, 50 percent of eight-to-twelve-year-olds, and 64 percent of thirteen-to-seventeen-year-olds have a set in their room.

Pete comes downstairs for a chocolate-chip cookie. He's been watching TV for an hour. And Vicky? Who knows? She's been holed up in her room since she came home from school. Americans today watch 50 percent more television than they did back in the 1950s. The TV set is now on an average of seven hours a day. On a winter weekday evening, more than half the population of the United States is watching television. The other day, Clarissa wondered how much TV, total, she's watched in her life. If she lives an average American life span, and watches the average amount of television, the answer is about seven years. Seven full years of your life. "This isn't a peculiarly American habit," John remarked. "Everybody, everywhere, watches TV." True. Every day on this planet, people watch an estimated 3.5 billion hours of television!

Scene II. Vicky's room.

Incredibly, Vicky, our all-American adolescent, is not on the phone at the moment. Her attention is fixed on her favorite show of the week. She never misses it. For that matter, she rarely misses her not-so-favorite shows. Yet, Vicky watches less television than most her age—only about thirty hours a week. Those hours do add up, though. By the time she is eighteen, will have spent more than twenty-three thousand hours in front of the TV, more than twice the eleven thousand hours she will have spent in the classroom.

Scene III. Little Pete's Room.

The bizarre aliens blasting way on the screen are among Pete's favorites. "Cool guns," he says. He needn't worry, though, about missing an explosion or two. Pete's only in the fourth grade, and can look forward to watching many more shoot-outs. According to a consensus of studies by research organizations that monitor television programs, by the time Pete graduates from elementary school, he will have seen more than a hundred thousand violent exchanges, including eight thousand murders. And he will feast on the gore during his four years in high school, when he will see another hundred thousand acts of violence and some fifty thousand murders. In addition, by the time he graduates high school, he will have watched 350,000 commercials.

Condemnations of television aren't new, but that doesn't make the concerns any less pressing. We know that people who watch lots of television have a skewed perception of the world in which they live; for example, while 13 percent of the population is "poor" according to the U.S. census, this group is represented by only 1.3 percent of the prime time characters on television. Heavy TV watchers are consistently found to think the world is scarier and more violent than it really is. Our immediate interest here, however, is television's lethal effect on the quality of our social and private leisure activities. Those effects are more pernicious than you might suppose.

Robert Putnam, a Harvard political scientist specializing in social behavior, described his project as "wrestling with a difficult mystery." As with all classic crime stories, this puzzle had clues waiting to be noticed and a cast of plausible suspects hovering nearby. This was the problem: Over the past several decades, the American participation in social activities—the nation's "social capital," as some call it—dropped precipitously and dramatically. Involvement in organizations decreased by 50 percent, social visiting was down by more than 35 percent, and for all the talk about religious revivals, Americans spend 30 percent less time in church than they did several decades ago. The decline cuts across the board, and is true among older citizens and younger citizens, men and women, blacks and whites. The drop was even more perplexing because other research shows a positive correlation between rising levels of education and increased social involvement. Yet during this period of reduced social activity, Americans were getting more educated than ever.

What gives? What is the cause of this extraordinary reduction in our social life?

Putnam sleuthed. He rounded up the usual suspects, interrogated each, and rejected them all. Among the potential causes he dismissed were:

- Increased mobility—but Americans are moving not more, but slightly less, than before.

- Increased time pressure—but we have more, not less, free time; full-time employees and part-timers are more involved in group activities than the unemployed, and housewives participate in community affairs even less than working women.

- Our messier family lives—but even happily married couples are less socially involved than before.

The signs pointed elsewhere for the answer. The culprit was television. Not only did the growth of television correspond precisely with the years of decline in social life, but other studies demonstrated a direct relationship between television viewing and reduced social involvement. Putnam's analysis of the data, which he recounts in his essay "The Strange Disappearance of Civic America," led him to conclude, "Television watching comes at the expense of nearly every social activity outside the home, especially social gatherings and informal conversations." This makes television unique. Other leisure activities don't inhibit social exchanges. Newspaper readers and book readers, for example, are more likely to be joiners than those who don't read. Activity and interests tend to breed more activity and interests—people who listen to classical music are more, not less, likely to attend ball games. But television watchers don't do much of anything else.

It gets worse. Sitting for hours in front of the TV set eats away at your psychological health, too. Prominent social psychologists are now convinced that the sharp rise in clinical depression in the United Stated is at least partially related to the rise in television viewing. When people are monitored after watching several hours of television, they are found to be less alert and more anxious than before; and this is true of adults, adolescents, and children. Moreover, the more you watch, the less you enjoy it. Passivity makes for despondency. (Are computers different? A 1998 study titled *Home Net*, conducted by Carnegie Mellon University, found significant increases in depression and loneliness among Internet users, but researchers have severely criticized the methodology of that study. While it is still too early to draw hard conclusions about the long-term effects of computer use, chat rooms are a definite form of socializing, and surfing the Web is assuredly more interactive than watching television.)

So why do we watch so much television? For starters, it's free and available. It's also familiar and undemanding. It takes just the push of a button. And it's habit-forming, too. For all these reasons, cutting down on your TV time is difficult. And, of course, cutting down does not mean eliminating entirely—certainly there's much on the tube that's excellent, entertaining, and enlightening. But if there's one thing you can do to bring you more free time, it's to overcome the temptation to watch. Unplug when you can. You'll be doing yourself—and the rest of your family—a grand favor.

This ends the homily on television and what not to do with your leisure time. Now comes the greater challenge: What to do with your leisure. How does leisure connect to our work and careers? The answer is already out there . . . and it directs us to look inward.

CREATING LEISURE

The Sabbath cannot survive in exile, a lonely stranger among days of profanity.

—Abraham Joshua Heschel

We need to reintroduce the Sabbath into our lives. Let me hasten to say that I don't mean the Sabbath as precisely defined in our religious traditions (that's your own business). This needn't be a calendar day, for that matter. I have in mind, rather, a period set aside for the personal nourishment and tranquillity that is the purpose of this day of rest. Our religious heritage, like every other, has its share of wisdom and folly, but we gave up too much when, in our rush to modernity, we jettisoned the concept of the Sabbath. This day can serve as a springboard, a framework, or if you prefer, a metaphor for rethinking what we want from our leisure time. Atheists need some Sabbath in their lives no less than the Amish or Orthodox Jews.

The biblical source for the Sabbath is brief but richly nuanced. The text suggests qualities that can help us shape our own contemporary approach to leisure.

Leisure blesses your work

He who clings to his work will create nothing that endures

WORK

If you want to accord with the Tao
Just do your job, then let go.

—Lao-tzu

The first essential feature of the Sabbath is its integral connection to work. You can't have one without the other. "Six days shall you labor and do all your work, and the seventh shall be a Sabbath for the Lord, your God" (Exodus 20:9–10). A life of work without repose is slavery. But leisure is not merely a break from work. It is also an affirmation of work. God blesses the seventh day as the completion of His creative work of the previous six days. This temporal division is a central theme in the religious orientation.

Humans continuously make distinctions about the world they live in, and according to the great nineteenth-century sociologist Emile Durkheim, the most basic distinction of all is between the sacred and the profane. All religions, therefore, delineate spaces that are designated as holy. These spaces typically have natural boundaries, such as bodies of water, caves, hilltops, and valleys. Time, on the other hand, has no natural distinctions, for one moment is just like the next, one twenty-four hour period no different from the one before or the one after. The innovation of religious time was to breach the continuity of the calendar by demarcating certain days as holy days, or as they've come to be called, holidays. The first time the word *holy* (*quodesh*) appears in the Bible, it is with regard to the seventh day, and the only time the word *holy* is used in the decalogue is the Fourth Commandment, enjoining us to remember the Sabbath and "keep it holy." The leisure of the Sabbath is sacred time.

We need intervals of leisure because work needs closure. This is why it is so important to segment long-term projects into assignments with definitive borders. Over the next two weeks, say, you decide that you need to finish this part of the document, this one sale, this paper, or this filing. How long should these work patches be? Long enough to make you feel like you've accomplished something substantial, but not so long that you become enslaved to your project. However, separating yourself from what you've produced can prove no less difficult than other separations in your life. Workaholics aren't people who work exceptionally long hours, but people who won't allow any of their tasks to terminate. And because they won't allow closure to their work life, many of them have trouble enjoying their retirement; they allow pieces of their past work to linger unresolved, gnawing at the leisure time for which they labored so many years.

Paradoxically, separation comes easiest when associated with creative work. When artists are done with a painting, carpenters finish constructing a room, writers end their book, or composers complete a piece of music, they commonly express an "odd sense of distance" from their product. Creative juices flowed during "the act of creation," but the work is now transformed into something that "was created." It stands on its own. The creation is complete when the goal is met and its purpose is fulfilled.

The worst thing about being unemployed, they say, it that you never get a day off. Weekends aren't as refreshing when you've had an unproductive week. The more creatively productive we are in our work, the greater the potential for leisure. In the biblical cosmogony, God has the ultimate creative week—He produced a universe, for God's sake—and so His closure, the Sabbath, is the ultimate leisure.

This explains, too, why slaves can rest but cannot have leisure. A slave does not decide when to begin his labor nor when to end it. Because the toil of slaves is not of their own choosing, the critical connection between leisure and work is absent. This relationship between autonomous work and leisure is explicit in the Bible. Scripture offers two different explanations for the command to keep the Sabbath. One is the notion of *imitatio dei*, of imitating God; as He created for six days and then ceased creation, so should we. The second explanation ties the Sabbath to the Exodus, the freeing of the Israelites from Egyptian bondage. The two accounts are, as we see, interconnected. Genuine leisure is possible only when the work you do freely originates from your own desires and ends when you decide it is complete.

This, then, is the first component of leisure. Without work there is no leisure. Work must sometime be brought to a close. When you are done with it, send it off to the world with your blessing, and take your leave of it. This begins your leisure.

Leisure is inward creation

To learn about oneself is to forget oneself.
                    —Dogen, Japanese Zen master

True happiness, we are told, consists in getting out of One's self but the point is not only to get out—you must stay out; and to stay out you must have some absorbing errand.

                    —Henry James

Leisure is not merely the cessation of work. Understandably, we need rest. Our strained bodies can use an extra hour of sleep, and some easy rocking in a hammock would be mighty fine. Our minds, too, need to be calmed after racing over our mental hurdles; a mindless flick, a junk novel, or some television might do the trick. But this is relaxation, not leisure.

Genesis describes the Sabbath as a positive creation in its own right. In the Hebrew text (though not in the Septuagint translation), God completes His endeavors not on the sixth but on the seventh day: "God had finished on the seventh day from all his work that he had made" (Genesis 2:2). What was created on this day? God created leisure, say the rabbis.

Leisure is a continuation of the creative process. In his book *The Human Shape of Work* sociologist Peter Berger explains that when we work, "we modify the world as it is formed," turn it into something it was not before.

Therefore, to work "is to mime creation itself." Satisfying, creative work is divine. And so is leisure. In our work we re-create the world. In our recreation that is leisure, we re-create ourselves. When work goes well, we help make the world run better. When our recreation goes well, we re-create ourselves: We reinvigorate our spirit, our enthusiasm, our beliefs, and the delicacy of our emotions.

Leisure is of a piece with work, and like it, flourishes when we are in the flow, free of the fetters of self-consciousness and external agendas. When we are with our friends, our purpose is just that—to be with our friends; we aren't selling product or buying applause. When we are by ourselves in our leisure, we are alone, but not lonely. We take long walks to reintroduce ourselves to our beliefs and feelings, and to try out new ideas and attitudes. We plant flowers, plaster the basement wall, concoct a new dish, practice a dance step, hone our old skills, and investigate new ones. It doesn't matter that our photographs, sketches, or flute playing will never be displayed on a museum wall nor performed in the concert hall, for the satisfaction is in the doing itself. So, too, alone or with others, we rejuvenate our bodies by hiking, taking a swim, attending a yoga class, or playing a game of chess. All this is leisure.

Leisure, we should emphasize, is not only a social or a physical activity. In leisure, our emotions get a workout, too. It is this emotional encounter in a leisure framework that explains how we can be so enthralled by a captivating book or piece of music, moved by a play or film.

Fictional worlds are safe. We enter them as participants,

knowing that what transpires is only pretend and soon to be over. We give up our self-consciousness and become actors in this game of make-believe: Our role is that of audience, and our reactions are part of the action. As with all leisure, the immediate point of the experience is the changes that happen within us, not on the outside. Here, in the safety zone of fiction, we exercise our emotions and unchain our feelings. We are free to weep, laugh, cringe, hope, imagine cruelty, and savor romance. In the refuge of the fairy tale, children explore their unspoken fear of monsters and villains. Young and old, we are eager to be transformed and transported by an imaginative tale, and that is why the majority of television programs are narratives. Fictional worlds afford us a break from the routine emotions of our everyday lives. We can sense that division when we walk out of the movie theater and the wave of the real world washes over us.

Some theorists advance the intriguing idea that leisure's sanctified space is also a central appeal of religious rituals. In the bounded space of the sanctuary, one partakes of a spiritual theater in which words and objects adopt special meanings and evoke a distinct feeling of devotion. From this perspective, religious practice is not like "ordinary world" work but a form of leisure, albeit intense and serious.

But discrimination matters. Junk art makes for junk leisure. Movies and music designed for quick profits make for cheap emotions. Repackaged genre books are cotton candy for the mind; they fill you up but they don't satisfy. Television laugh tracks badger us to chuckle, but the smile belongs to others. Biologist George Klein, in his book of essays, *Live Now*, calls the offerings of popular culture "parasites of our psyches," for they "absorb our mental energy but provide no strength in return." This is no elitist prejudice. A thriller on the beach is sometimes just the right read, and an occasional Whopper at Burger King is a lark. The sorrow is that for so many of us, "sometimes" and "occasionally" have increasingly become routine. The heavy stamp of "culture" attaches to a visit to an art gallery, to an hour of concentrated listening to a Beethoven concerto, to watching a ballet or an independent "art" movie, to reading a Shakespeare sonnet. We want to enjoy our leisure, not exhibit our virtue, and so we "never get around" to these more fulfilling experiences. The loss is ours.

No one should dictate to others how to enrich their passions or refine their sensibilities. But, as elsewhere, discriminating taste in one's leisure brings deeper delights. And delight is a basic component of leisure.

Leisure is about joy

The sages interpreted the commandment "Thou shalt not kindle a fire throughout your habitations on the Sabbath day" (Exodus 35:3) as also meaning "Thou shalt not kindle a fire of controversy nor the heat of anger." Indeed, this is a day not for fire but to "chill."

According to Jewish tradition, married couples are encouraged to have sex on the Sabbath. In the Cabala, the Sabbath is personified as a bride and the People as the groom—marital intimacy parallels this cosmic union; we describe great sex as divine. But the more straightforward reason for having sexual relations on the Sabbath is that the day is designated for wholesome, joyous leisure.

We've forgotten how to feel good about feeling good. We feel compelled to justify our play by turning it into an instrument for other aims, such as health or education. The suggestion that we have lost our appreciation of pleasure will strike many as incredible. We are more accustomed to the relentless rant of our self-appointed moralists about how America has become the bastion of corrupt hedonism, a nation devoted solely to gratification. These preachers miss the point. The shame is not that we care too much about pleasure but that we care too little. We satisfy ourselves with crumbs of commercial entertainment. We amuse ourselves momentarily, thinly. Pleasure, too, needs cultivation.

The nation's puritanical strain harks back to our Puritan origins. The killjoys within our religious traditions even managed to kill the joy of the Sabbath/Sunday. Declaring merriment unseemly, they forbade public dancing, deemed group singing sinful, and transformed the day created for delight into a day of solemn self-denial.

Wanton gambling and drunken carnivals are, to be sure, unsatisfactory pleasures. We certainly don't need to submerge into the debased thrills that sometimes mistakenly pass for leisure. The citizens of ancient Rome, for example, spent their mornings at the Colosseum, enjoying the spectacle of mortal combat between gladiators and fights to the death between slaves and wild animals. The crowd broke for lunch and returned for the afternoon fare of capital punishments that typically included crucifying some hapless fellow and then dragging him around the arena while beating him to death with rods. In the games directed by Emperor Trajan, nine thousand animals were killed and scores of condemned criminals were tied to stakes perched on platforms and set upon by starved carnivores. The audiences loved it.

This is revelry, not true leisure. Self-indulgence is appropriate when you indulge those parts of your self that you esteem and believe deserve cultivation. Pandering to your streaks of cruelty hardly qualifies. Less obviously, we need to ask what aspect of ourselves is attracted to the blandishments of most mass entertainment. Are we happy with the returns we get for spending so much of our time as the audience for its products? Be selfish with your leisure. Don't squander it on activities that have nothing to do with the self that matters to you most.

What you do with your leisure is your business in the most literal sense of the term. Your business, we've said, is your life; and, indeed, how you live it is your business. Your leisure is critical to your work and life, and therefore must reflect your personal aspirations. Here are three suggestions that we all might usefully bear in mind as we develop our individual leisure interests.

■ Take your play seriously.

Understanding physics is child's play compared to understanding child's play.

—Albert Einstein

The "fun" of playing, resists all analysis, all logical inter-
pretation . . . [as] a concept, it cannot be reduced to any
other mental category.

—Johan Huizinga

Leisure, we've argued, is the internal complement of our external work. It makes sense, therefore, to use your leisure time to explore aspects of yourself that you neglect in the course of your work. For example, if your job requires concentrated analysis and rigorous thinking, spend some leisure time nourishing the "other side of your brain." Cater to your romantic sensibilities: Dance slowly to the riffs of sensual jazz and rediscover the joys of a passionate kiss . . . or the equivalent for you. If you talk, sell, or administer for a living, why not quiet the chatter during your free time? Go for a leisurely walk, mess with those watercolors, read. If your brain is largely on hold during your work hours—you manage papers and forms all day, say—you might want to exercise your thinking during your leisure by solving puzzles, playing thought games, learning a new language, or writing fiction. But all our leisure should have the element of play—taking chances with ourselves, delighting in discovering the unexpected about ourselves.

The nature of economies, particularly in our contemporary world, entails specialization. Our jobs demand that we concentrate on distinct skills; our other interests and talents, in the meantime, lie fallow and unattended. We can restore that balance in our leisure. We are thinking beings with imaginative and spiritual yearnings centered by our bodies that demand exertion and rest. We need an occasional round of waltzing and sensual stroking. We should laugh a lot more and sometimes cry more, too. We need our friends, and they need us. Our job can't provide all this by itself, nor can our leisure. But by integrating work with leisure, the totality of our lives is broadened and enriched.

- Do, don't just watch.

One trend that has remained steady the past few decades is the turn of Americans from activists to spectators. Increasingly, we spend our free time observing other people at play and work. Watching a ball game, listening to music, or reading is certainly fun and, on occasion, even inspiring, but it is not a substitute for playing ball, playing an instrument, or writing. Maybe you can't sing as well as Barbra Streisand, but it will be *your* singing. You can't write a screenplay as well as Spielberg? So what? This is *your* screenplay. If leisure is about internal creativity, you can't spend all of it consuming other people's creativity. You might be surprised by what you can do.

Philosophers often employ a *gedankenexperiment,* a thought experiment, to extrapolate the core of some issue or principle. These sci-fi hypotheses help illuminate problems in everything from theoretical physics to ethics and values. The approach also sheds light on what's important in our leisure.

Imagine, if you will, that the president of the United States appears on television looking harried and grim.

He announces that a massive asteroid is set to crash into the Earth in ten days, causing the end of life on this planet. There is nothing anyone can do to deter the impending catastrophe. This is the cliché plotline of summer films, but a useful exercise nonetheless. Disregarding the inevitable panic that would follow this information, the collapse of social services and enforcement of safety, how would you spend those ten remaining days?

You wouldn't keep your appointment for a haircut. You wouldn't bother completing your memo or term paper that's due next week. Nor would you spend the time as an impassive couch potato watching television. You'd probably get together for many hours with family and friends. You'd listen to the music you love most. You'd talk to your god and to yourself, and take a trip to the beach to stand in front of the ocean at twilight. You'd reach down deep inside and try doing those things you've promised yourself you'd get to later in your life. (Notice, by the way, that the time with friends, the walks, the thoughts, most of the activities most essential to you don't cost any money.)

These are your core leisure activities. We can't live our lives as though they will end tomorrow. Nor should we—tomorrow is sure to come, and we need to be prepared for it when it arrives. Moreover, some of our most enriching leisure pastimes require years of practice. But we also manage to let life's habit overrun us, lose our sense of proportion, and delay forever the moments that mean the most to us.

Why reserve your best leisure for the last fifteen or twenty years of your life? Leisure, like work, is a lifetime activity, changing and developing as we change and develop. Our leisure time is limited. It is not infinitely replenished. Given the time you have, how do you want to spend it? What would you most miss not having done? Make that determination, and then make that activity a part of your leisure.

We noted that creative work and creative leisure are complementary, each part of a larger whole. But even more: Thriving in one sector inspires us to do better in the other. Creativity is self-rewarding and self-propelling; when we are re-creative in our leisure, we are more creative in our work, and vice versa. So, too, when we enlarge our sense of responsibility for our careers, we are more eager to accept responsibility for our leisure, and vice versa. And both our work and leisure need to flourish if we are to succeed in our entrepreneurial-careers.

Your Brilliant Career

AMERICANS have many faults, but laziness at work isn't one of them. (On the other hand, as we saw, when it comes to leisure, we are horrendously and unhappily lazy.) We are willing to put in the long hours at our jobs, willing to take chances, learn new skills, and to look to the future. But we're no longer sure why we should.

As we noted, work ethics were traditionally embedded in some theological frameworks, but the call to work as a service to God or as the route to individual salvation no longer inspires us. The formerly dominant Protestant work ethic, especially in its Puritan guise, strikes us as impossibly dour and unappealing. The Marxist celebrations of the proletariat ring hollow. At the same time, we know that our insatiable craving for the luxuries hawked in the marketplace can't justify all the effort we put into our labor. Where, then, do we look to justify spending so much of our life at work?

The incentive for work, I've suggested, will emerge from the work itself. It will be found in work that derives from our individual choices and satisfies our creative aspirations. And this kind of work will transform our careers.

We will need to start thinking of ourselves as career

entrepreneurs. Here, in summary, is what that transformation will entail.

- Our skills and knowledge are the products we bring to the marketplace. Therefore, we no longer will *have* a job, we will *do* a job. It could be a ten-week gig or a fifteen-year project, but in either case we are selling a service, not contracting for lifetime employment.

- We no longer have a boss. Our boss is our client. We are vendors of our skills, and our "boss" and the organization he or she represents has purchased our talent. Therefore, we can't be fired. Sure, we can get a pink slip tomorrow and have no place to work the day after. But we should regard the dismissal as having lost a client, perhaps our most important client; clients come and go. By the same token, we can fire our client—previously, this was called quitting. Either way, we should see it is as a relationship that didn't work out.

- Our deepest career commitment must be to the work itself. Our skills and our personal network are what we need to lean on now. Therefore, we can forget job security. We can forget job loyalty. We can't rely on either any longer. Neither we nor the organization for which we work owes the other permanent allegiance.

- The work life vs. private life dichotomy is over. Our personal life includes our work, and our work includes our personal life. When things go well, the two form a seamless unity. Skills quickly become obsolete, and education is now an ongoing process. When you grow as a person, your career is enriched, and as your career develops, so do you.

■ And, therefore, "making it" is now ours to define. Without job titles or a ready-made ladder of promotions, we will have no objective criteria by which to judge how we are doing. But we need to be prepared: Living without external yardsticks is unsettling and more difficult than most imagine. We will need huge doses of courage and conviction.

Does this prognosis sound overheated, exaggerated? Not if you work in graphic design, editing, catering, advertising, computer technology, most segments of the entertainment business, or any other industry in which working project by project, client by client, is already the norm. But you may not think this scenario applies to you if you have an established job in an established company: You're pretty sure, at least for now, that your job has a future; you're damn sure that you have a boss; and you have no doubt that, call it what you will, getting fired is getting fired.

You might be right . . . for the moment. The metamorphosis of the workplace isn't uniform across all industries, and some traditional job trajectories will continue for some time. Many current executives will make it to retirement, most postal workers will, university professors can relax on their cushy tenured mattress, and you, too, may survive until you get your gold watch. Just don't count on it. Job security is dwindling in every business, and when reality ups and rears its unpleasant surprises, those who least expect to be let go are always the most bewildered. The trappings of security are just that . . . a trap.

The demise of the job is scary. The safety net is gone. The burden of acquiring benefits, pensions, and health care now falls on your own financial shoulders. Many will suffer—economic shifts are always painful—and the security that comes with a traditional job can't easily be replaced even by the most upbeat rhetoric. But pain is just one side of the coin—transformations are also opportunities. Having your livelihood suddenly depend on your own initiative is frightening, but it also can be liberating; what you lose in financial assurance, you gain in personal integrity. Most people never determine what they themselves consider success or failure, but simply adopt the prevalent markers of the culture they live in. In the new entrepreneurial-career, the criteria for making it are no longer clear-cut; the old notions no longer apply, so you must establish your own definitions of success.

As I've noted, the determination to develop one's own definition of success and failure requires that we draw on all the courage we can muster. We can't afford to be lulled by empty slogans, no matter how momentarily uplifting—intellectual honesty and rigor will be critical in forming our personal visions. The careers we create for ourselves will contour the lives we create for ourselves, and "doing a life" isn't easy. But the potential rewards will certainly make the effort worth it. No longer must we choose between making a living and making a life. We can make a living *and* make a life. We should not settle for less.

Index

Competition, destructiveness of, 106–16

Complaining about jobs, 38, 39

Compliments, deflecting, 165

Compromise, 47–48

Consumer treadmill, 127

Contentment and success, 95–96

Contrast principle, 39–40

Cooperation and rewards, 77

Cooperative competition, 114–15

Courage and creativity, 33

Coyne, James, on self-validation, 164

Creativity
  entrepreneur, 31–33
  leisure and, 201–4
  performance and, 110–11

Crisp, Quentin, on money and happiness, 123

Csikszentmihalyi, Mihaly, on flow, 88–89, 90–91

Culbert, Samuel A., on leadership, 136

Culture
  entrepreneurs and heritage, 15–16
  leisure and, 203–4

cummings, e. e., on being yourself, 105

Curiosity and motivation, 82–83, 91

Curse, work as, 19

Davenport, Rita, on money, 122

deChalmes, Richard, on autonomy, 87

Deci, Robert, on rewards and motivation, 72–73

Deming, W. Edwards, on Total Quality Management, 12–13

Depression, 195–96

Differences in aspirations, 48

Distortions about work, 51–64

Dogen, on learning about oneself, 201

Dressing for work, 148

Drucker, Peter
  on executive versus management, 13

on knowledge workers, 134–35
  on profit motive, 53

Duell, Charles H., on inventions, 31

Durkheim, Emile, on the sacred and profane, 198

Durocher, Leo, on losers, 106

Dweck, Carol, on expectations editing reality, 156–57

Earhart, Amelia, on soloing, 5

Edison, Thomas, on failure, 31

Efficiency of leisure, 189–90

Effort as success. *See* Journey

Einstein, Albert
  on play, 206
  theory of relativity, 169–70

Elasticity of money, 125, 126

Eliot, George, on self-confidence, 165

Emerson, Ralph Waldo, on cost of money, 128

Emotional workout, leisure, 202–3

Employment at will, 57

Empowerment, 13

End of Ideology, The (Bell), 19

Ends into means, 81

Enjoyment trap, 24–26

Entrepreneurs, 3–33
  calling, predestined, 21–24
  Calvinist work ethic, 18
  career entrepreneurs, ix–xi, 28–33, 211–14
  Catholic work ethic, 18–19
  challenge from work, 27–28
  choosing careers, 23–25
  Christian work ethic, 16–17, 17–18
  courage and creativity, 33
  creativity, 31–33
  cultural heritage impact, 15–16
  curse, work as, 19
  empowerment, 13
  enjoyment trap, 24–26
  family impact, 14
  global economy impact, 7–8

Index

gratification, 26–27
Greek work ethic, 16
history, 4–14
humor and creativity, 33
industrialization impact, 6
informated workplace, 9
insecurity, 6
inspiration, 32
meaningful work, 20–28
mergers, 8
moral consciousness and work, 19
other-directed work, 20
outsourcing, 8
passion and creativity, 33
personality of, 29
philosophy, 15–20
pieceworkers, 5–6
postindustrial world, 6–7
process, commitment to, 29–30
project as supreme, 10
Protestant work ethic, 18
scientific management (Taylorism),
    11–12, 13–14
"secret of life," 4
security, 6, 8
self-directed work, 20, 21
shuushin koyoo seido, 7
talent trap, 24
task-oriented work, 5
technology impact, 8–10
Total Quality Management, 12–13
women's impact, 14
work defined, 15
workers' attitude, 10–14
work ethic, need for new, 3–4
See also Leisure; Living versus life;
    Motivation; Self-confidence;
    Success
Envy, self-understanding from,
    98–105
Envy and Originality (Van Kamm),
    105
Epictetus, on contentment, 95
Epstein, Jason, on money, 122

Ethics of Authenticity, The (Taylor), 81
Expectations about jobs, 39–41
Expectations editing reality, 156–57
External motivation, 73–75

Family impact, 14
Fast Company magazine, 47
Fear, power for instilling, 132
Fear of failure, 157–59
Feelings: Our Vital Signs (Gaylin),
    102
Fictional worlds for leisure, 202–3
Fischer, Bobby, on optimism, 157
Flow, going with, 88–92
Flow (Csikszentmihalyi), 88
Fox, Matthew, on Christianity and
    work, 17–18
Freud, Sigmund
    on money, 122
    on work, reality attachment from,
    1

Gauguin, Paul, on moral obligations,
    142–43
Gaylin, Willard, on envy, 102
Gedankenexperiment, 208–9
General Electric Corporation, 58
Get Better or Get Beaten! (Slater), 58
Getty, J. P., on success, 5
Gilgorich, Thomas, on self-
    assessment, 151
Gill, Diane L., on competition in
    sports, 111
Global economy impact, 7–8
Godbey, Geoffrey, on time overload,
    189
Goethe, Johann Wolfgang von, on
    growth, 137
Goldschmidt, Walter, on prestige,
    137
*Grace of Great Things: Creativity
    and Innovation, The* (Grudin),
    32
Gratification, 26–27

Index

Index

Index

Index

Index

Index